Book One
1955 – March 1972

Chapter One

My Senior Year

I grew up thinking I was the dumbest kid in the world. I suppose most of my friends today would still think, "and yes, your still the dumbest kid in the world too!!" It might have helped though, if I had studied a little bit in school. It might have helped more even if I had stayed, inside the school! I remember during Agriculture class—Ag class as we called it—the teacher, Mr Olson, would have several of us go into the cloak room during the last thirty minutes of class to study grain, leaves and wood samples. We'd be in there a few minutes and then we'd open a window. A couple of us would jump out and walk a block east to a little grocery store and get pop and candy bars for everyone. Then we'd walk back to school, climb in the window and drink pop and eat candy bars! How we ever did that all year without getting, caught, has always amazed me!

Cloquet High School

I remember one especially beautiful fall day, when I just couldn't make myself go back to school after lunch. (actually, I guess there were quite a few days like that!) I hiked to the west side of town and hitchhiked home. I walked into the house and, boy, was my mother mad! I said, "Gee's Mom, it ain't like I'm flunking anything. It was just too nice out to go back to school after lunch, and besides I want to go partridge hunting." She said, "Well, it wouldn't be so bad if just one of you skipped school, but your older brother just came home a half hour ago and he's out hunting already!" (Hmmm, I figured, it ain't my fault then, must run in the family!")

A few days later I got home from school, on the bus this time, and got ready to go partridge hunting. My Dad said, "How's about sticking around and helping me dig the sewer line!" He was putting in inside plumbing, and we were going to dig it in all by hand, including the septic tank and the drain field. We had just gotten the sewer pipe outside the house and had an open trench about 15 feet long and 8 feet deep right along the house. I said, "Gee dad, I want to go partridge hunting for awhile. I'll help you when I get back." I hunted for an hour and half, missed a couple, and came home. As I walked up, my dad said, "How did you do?" I said, "I missed a couple." He lifted up his shovel, which had a dead partridge on it, and said, "I get more partridges with a shovel, than you get with a shotgun!" A partridge had flown between the apple trees in the yard and smacked into the house right above my dad and fell dead, into the trench at his feet!

I don't think I ever took a book home. In my senior year I'd get out of school at 3:45, hurry down to the Match Mill, punch in by 4:00, and drive a Clark forklift on the shipping crew, loading boxcars, etc. until midnight. Joe Thill Sr.was the manager in charge of the warehouse and shipping crew. There were only three of us on the "four to midnight" shift, me another kid, and an "older guy," probably in his 30s. (That was "old" to me back then when I was 18!)

Joe must not have heard anything about a couple of us kids having drag races and playing chase on those forklifts after he left. One night I was chasing the other kid around out in the warehouse, which was full of boxes of matches on pallets, from the floor to as high as we could stack them–20 feet maybe. He made a 90 degree left turn down one of the aisles, I came around the corner, in hot pursuit, and the forklift started sliding sideways a little. My right fork sliced through one of those boxes of matches, and POOF, the whole box was on fire!

My first thought was, "Oh shit, I'm going to burn the whole mill down!" Luckily we had fire extinguishers on the forklifts, so I grabbed it and extinguished the fire before it spread!

Thinking back on it now, I would guess that in another five seconds, the fire would have accelerated to a point where it would have been out of control and unstoppable! Can you imagine starting a fire in a warehouse full of matches?! My "hot pursuit" had just about gotten "hot enough" to burn the mill down! That must have been one of the first times that God looked down on me and thought, "Look at that dumb kid. I better help him before he burns the whole mill down and puts 450 people out of work!" We quit racing out in the warehouse after that.

Joe would always stop and talk to me about 5 o'clock on his way out of the mill, as I was sitting on the forklift waiting for the pallet to get stacked full of boxes. He would tell me where he wanted me to stack pallets of boxes in the warehouse or what he wanted taken out of the warehouse and put into boxcars, etc. He never came right out and said anything about drag racing and playing chase though. As he was leaving, he'd always pat that Clark forklift, on the "rump" and say, "Remember Hubbell, you're driving two Cadillac's there." I'd say, "Right Joe."

After work I'd stop at Jim's Hamburgers and have a "sloppy Joe" and a malt and get home about 1:15. The next day on the way to study hall, which was a very large room with a stage on one end and a teacher sitting up on the stage, I'd stop by the library and check out the biggest book I could find. I'd set it up on my desk--in a "V" so it'd stand up by itself--way in the back row and slump down and take a nap for about 45 minutes. Never got caught the whole year either!

After a couple of months, the other kid and I noticed that the third driver, the "older guy", would disappear about 9 P.M., and we wouldn't see him again until quitting time. So we asked him one night, "Where do you go, have you got another job in the mill or what? He said, "I guess I can trust you guys now, so I'll show you."

We followed him out into the warehouse. We climbed up some concrete stairs and about halfway up we got off on the right. We were about 10 feet up, on top of the boxes of matches stacked there. We went about 12 feet and he removed a couple of the boxes from under the stairs, and showed us, "his room!"

He had a room about eight feet wide and ten feet long under the stairs!! The floor was covered with blankets. He had a sleeping bag, a reading light, some magazines, pop and chips! I couldn't believe it!! After that though, we took turns using, "the room" when things slowed up enough where two guys could manage! I only used it a couple of times when I'd had a long night before and didn't get a good nap in "study hall." I enjoyed driving that Clark forklift anyway.

Being number five out of ten kids on a farm west of Cloquet, Minnesota, I knew college wasn't an option for me. In fact, I can remember thinking that college was just for the smart and rich kids and I figured "I ain't neither one of those."

Nobody ever sat down with me and said, "Les, what do you want to do for a living after school?" My only plan for after school was, "how can I get my girlfriend in the back

Author in his 1936 Cadillac.

seat of my 1936 Cadillac!?" That's about how far my planning went back then!

I had my application in at all three of the mills in Cloquet. After I graduated in 1955, the Wood Conversion Company called me one day and offered me a job. They paid maybe 20 cents an hour more than the Match Mill, so I quit the Match Mill and went to work there. Then a couple of months later the Paper Mill called me. They paid another 25 cents more, so I quit the Wood Conversion and went to work there. If you were going to work in Cloquet, the Paper Mill paid the most.

My dad worked there for about thirty-five years or more, before he retired. I was at the Paper Mill for only about two months when I met a guy who had been working there for twenty years. He was making about $350 a month. I had just started, and I was making about $350 a month! I got to thinking about that and I thought, "I'll be damned if I want to work here for twenty years and have some kid come along and start out at the same money as I'm making!

Chapter Two

Basic Training

So I joined the Air Force. I went to Duluth and got on a train heading for San Antonio, Texas. The train stopped in Minneapolis and a kid got on and sat next to me. His name was, Melvin Johnson, come to think of it, it still is Melvin Johnson! He'd grown up on a farm in Erwin, South Dakota. We were two farm kids so we had a lot in common. In fact this was going to be the farthest from home either of us had ever been.

We were really naive about the rest of the world! I've never forgotten what happened when we got to San Antonio and got off the train. They put all, of the forty or so of us into a little room to wait for the bus to take us out to Lackland Air Force base. It was about 3:30 in the morning. Now this was the first time Johnson and I had ever seen "colored" kids up close. I had seen a couple of them walking the streets of Duluth the few times I had been down there. These colored kids were walking around like chickens walk, saying, "muvfer fug" this and "muvfer fug" that. I asked Johnson, "Can you understand what they're saying?" He couldn't; and I couldn't either.

Pretty soon the bus showed up and we were taken to the base. They dumped us off at a barracks at about 5 A.M. and we just went in and lay down on those old army cots and went to sleep.

About 8 A.M. though, we heard a Chinese sergeant hollering for us "rainbows" to hit the deck and "fallout out front on the street." (They called us rainbows because of all the different colored clothes we had on.) He told us in no uncertain terms that he was our TI (training instructor) and that it was his job to make men out of us miserable excuses for human beings. He said, "Before I'm done you'll hate my guts!" I thought about telling him, that I'd just met him and I hated his guts already, but I sensed that he might not appreciate my sense of humor, so I let it slide.

Besides, he was already chewing out some kid for just looking at him! And if you even smiled he was right in your face, "What are you smiling at rainbow, do you think something is funny boy, let's see if you're smiling when you're cleaning the latrine at ten o'clock tonight rainbow!"

Then he marched us down the barber shop and they sheared us like sheep!! We looked like a bunch of cue balls! Some of those guys were about to cry because they had lost their "identity". And that's why they do it, to make us all equal so we can be molded into the Air Force's way of thinking and doing things.

Next he marched us over to the have our flight physicals etc. I had to go out in the hall and drink as much water as I could so I'd weigh enough to make the 100 pound minimum to join! Then it was next door to get our uniforms and back to the barracks. There you learned how to make your bed with hospital corners etc., so he could bounce a quarter off it! I thought, "Who the hell cares if a quarter will bounce when it hits the bed or not!" My mother never bounced a quarter off my bed! She never chewed me out even, for not making my bed. And I don't think I ever did make it! But this TI guy had a "thing" for bouncing quarters off beds and I thought, "I bet he likes to go down to the river and listen to the bridge rust too!" Somebody was always getting his ass chewed for some little thing, so I learned fast that this was going to be a good time to not stand out in the crowd.

After the bed-making lesson, he said "fallout on the street!" He formed us into six rows of maybe eight guys in a row according to height. And then we were learning how to march! What a joke that was at first! I didn't know anything about marching. He chewed my ass once. He was nose to nose with me and said, "What do you think you are boy, a storm trooper? I said march, not gooseneck!" One morning, about a week later, he had us out on the parade field marching. Of course we didn't have this marching down too good yet, and he brought us to a halt and said, "You guys are supposed to be the cream of the crop. You look more like the 'jackoff' to me!" I'll bet those TIs would have some good laughs at the beer garden every night sharing the lines they had come up with! Pretty soon we got better and the TI became almost civil.

I liked the obstacle course. It was like being back on the farm! What you had to do was climb a rope up a fifty foot cliff, crawl through some culverts, run through tires, crawl up and over fences, catch a rope and swing across a twenty foot mud puddle about two feet deep, walk a rope "bridge" about twenty feet in the air between two trees, and end up back in the staging area.

This was just like everything we did back on the farm so I thought it was great fun! In fact I passed up the squad leader going up the rope and was back in the staging area before most guys got to the top of the cliff! The TI said, "You think you're pretty good don't you!?" Before I could think, I said, "I'll take you through." Not what he wanted to hear! He said, "Give me a hundred push-ups!" Hell, I could do push-ups all day back then, so I gave him 150!

In fact, before I was done with basic training he called me into his office and wanted to know if I'd stay and be a TI. I was just a shy, bashful farm kid, much as I am today, and didn't see myself chewing some poor young airmen's asses all day and half the night, so I respectfully declined. Anyway, I made it through basic, no worse for the experience!

When you join the Air Force, they give you all kinds of tests. It turned out I had a aptitude in both "electrical and mechanical." My ambition at that time was, maybe I could be a crew chief on something, so I chose mechanical. I knew I was too dumb to be a pilot.

Chapter Three

Tech school

After basic training, they sent Johnson and me to Sheppard Air Force Base in Wichita Falls, Texas to go to "mechanics school" on a C124 Globemaster. At first we were in a PAT (Personnel Awaiting Training) squadron for two-three weeks. Then we moved into another barracks to go to school.

The first day we were there we had a day off and got passes, and Johnson and I went to town. I've never forgotten the signs some people had in their yards, "Dogs and Airmen, keep off the grass." ("And here I was going to be protecting them," I thought!)

When we got to town, we had a few beers, I bought a new light brown suede jacket, we did some sightseeing, had a few more beers and caught a bus back to the base. When we got back to the base, we got off at the club, and of course, had a few more beers. It was dark and raining lightly when we left the club. About four or five of us were walking back to our new barracks, laughing, hollering, singing, etc. There were these little white picket fences on each corner and someone said, "Hubbell, I bet you can't jump that fence!" I said, "The hell I can't" and started running. I guess I jumped about six feet too soon and tripped over the fence and rolled in the mud. We got back to the barracks and we vomited all over the bathroom.

I had a hell of a time climbing the stairs. I still remember that it looked like those stairs were about three miles long and very steep. I sat on the bottom steps for awhile wondeing how the hell I was going to get upstairs. Finally we somehow got up there, tripped over a few footlockers, made a lot of noise, and woke up a bunch of guys. They were hollering and swearing at us, but we finally made it to our bunks on the far end of the barracks. I remember thinking, "These guys ain't very hospitable."

The next morning the barracks chief had us up early cleaning up the latrine. That wasn't so bad, but I had also ruined my new jacket that I had just paid $24.99 for too! Johnson figured we just weren't very good at making good first impressions.

LAST NAME - FIRST - MIDDLE INITIAL				GRADE	COURSE			CLASS
HURDELL LESLIE V				A/3C	AE43131E-1			0F026
36. ACTION								
ASSIGNED TO	CLASS NO	SHIFT	PAR	SO	DATE	REASON		
3792 STU SQ 3750 TTW	0F026		11 232					
						A/N PRESENTED LTR OF XE COMMENDATION BY BASE COMDR		
VD 12 June 56			6 Par 81		6 June 56	AWD PAFSC 43131R CHANNEL C-124		

37. PHASE TITLE	38. HOURS	39. PERFORM TEST SCORE	40. WRITTEN TEST SCORE	41. PHASE AVERAGE SCORE	37. PHASE TITLE	38. HOURS	39. PERFORM TEST SCORE	40. WRITTEN TEST SCORE	41. PHASE AVERAGE SCORE
A/C MECH FUND FOR MECH PWR PLT & PWR PLT SYST	120	65	69	66					
PWR PACK UP CHARGE FLT CONT SURF & SYST & AIRFRAMES	120	59	73	63					
ELECT FUND AND FUND UTILITY & LAND GEAR SYSTEM	120	65	59	63					
INSP & MAINT A/C SUPPT EQUIP CHANNEL C-124	150	71	65	69					

42. REPEAT CASES			INTERPRETATION OF PHASE TEST SCORES		43. TOTAL HOURS	44. FINAL GRADE
42A NO OF PH RPT	42B. CRSE AVG BASED ON ORIG PH SCORES		65 AND ABOVE - HIGHEST (7%) 45-54 - AVERAGE (38%) 55-64 - ABOVE AVERAGE (24%) 35-44 - BELOW AVERAGE (24%) 34 AND BELOW - LOWEST (7%)		510	65
45. REMARKS						
					Julian D Butler	
45A. TRANSFERRED TO	PAR	SO	DATE	46. CERTIFICATION (Signature)		
PARKS AFB, CALIF.	r	108	63	JULIAN D BUTLER, ASST USAF, STU REC OFF		

Much to our surprise, Johnson and I were always first, second or third in our class. In fact they had us tutoring other kids! I remember thinking, "Maybe I ain't the dumbest kid in the world, maybe I'm about the twentieth dumbest kid

Certificate of ACHIEVEMENT

TECHNICAL TRAINING AIR FORCE   USAF TECHNICAL SCHOOL

For outstanding performance of academic duties while attending a course of technical instruction at the United States Air Force Technical School at ___SHEPPARD___ Air Force Base.

___AIRMAN THIRD CLASS MELVIN E JOHNSON   AF 17 450 584___

led his class with a scholastic average of ___66___ in the ___AB43131B-1___ Course. His technical ability and earnest application reflect great credit upon himself. He is hereby commended for this notable achievement.

JULIAN G BUTLER
1STLT, USAF
School Secretary

EDWARD H WHITE
MAJOR GENERAL, USAF
Wing Commander

FORM 32
7 MAR 56

Air Force-Keesler AFB, Miss/K6-864

in the world!" Well, we surprised ourselves and got through school! In fact Johnson graduated first in the class and I was second! Not bad for a couple of farm kids, we figured!!

They made us a couple of 43131B's, which was the designation given to "two engines or more reciprocating engine mechanics" and cut us orders to go to Kadena AFB, Okinawa. Boy, we thought we were "hot shit!" Fresh off the farm--first to Texas, and now to Okinawa! We were becoming a couple of world travelers!! Hell, I hadn't even known where Texas was, let alone Okinawa!

We went home for a thirty day leave and I got married. The wife had a 1951 Ford, so we drove that to Niagara Falls, New York, on our honeymoon.

About fifty miles west of Niagara Falls, on a two lane winding road, I caught up to a dump truck and couldn't pass him for at least five miles! Finally I saw my chance and I dropped that Ford into second gear and got around him just before the next corner! About an hour later we arrived in Niagara Falls and I slowed up and shifted down to second as we approached the first stop sign. The only problem was that now second gear was going "klunk, klunk, klunk!" I had broken a tooth off second gear when I downshifted behind that truck! We found a motel within walking distance of the Falls so we wouldn't have to drive anyplace. The first day we were content to just stay in our room and relax after the trip, etc., etc., etc., etc., with a walk to view the falls and to the hamburger stand, now and then.

The next day I made some calls to the local junkyards and found a transmission. I negotiated a $30 trade with the lady who owned the yard. She loaned me some tools, and one of her men for ten minutes to help get the transmission lined up and back in place. All together it took me less than two hours to change out that transmission! It was a good thing I was a farm kid and knew how to do that or we might not have had enough money to get back home!

Chapter Four

"Shipping out"

I was married for fifteen days and then reported to Parks AFB in Sacramento, California to ship out for Okinawa. We were going to be there for about five to seven days. Every morning we'd fall out, as they called it out there too, and the first sergeant would call role call and pick about 40 of us young airmen, out of the maybe 150 there, to do different duties on the base. I told Johnson, "Stick with me and we won't do shit while we're here." Every day we'd stand where the sergeant had picked guys the day before, and sure enough, "We didn't do shit while we were there."

As soon as we were dismissed, we'd go down to the Airmen's Club, drink beer, and smoke cigarettes. (I don't think Johnson smoked though, he wasn't as cool as me – probably smarter though.) Then we'd play those crane machines, the ones where you put a quarter in and then you have about a minute of time to try and pick up a prize and drop it into the chute. We about went broke doing that but we had a lot of fun!

There was another one of us, "young airmen" there. He would watch us. We always figured he was about "a quart low." A couple of times he told us, "You guys would be good crane operators." "Right!" we said.

Finally we shipped out on the "Gaffee" to Okinawa. Everyone aboard ship had to do some kind of duty so I told Johnson, "Stick with me and raise your hand when I do." After a bit, the sergeant asked for two volunteers. My, "keeping out of work" instinct said "this is it", so I raised my hand and Johnson raised his hand, and the sergeant said, "Report to the bakery!" Johnson and I laughed all the way there!

We reported to a black sergeant baker, who was a really nice guy. I think he figured Johnson and I were going to screw up more than do any good while we were assigned to

Above: Lovelett, Hubbell on the railing, and Presol in Yokohama harbor

Below: Our view of Formosa from the Gaffee

help him so we'd report in
and he'd send us on our
way! It was the nicest cruise
I've ever been on! Come to
think of it, it's the only
cruise I've ever been on!

I'm beginning to think,
I really like being in the Air
Force! It was the best thing
I had ever done I figured,
except for marrying my high
school sweetheart!

We rode out a typhoon
someplace off Formosa.
Everybody on the ship was

Johnson on Gaffee in
Yokahama harbor

seasick except me I think. We were supposed to stay inside,
but I couldn't stand the smell of all these guys vomiting so I
went out on the back end, or stern as it was called. The captain must have been just keeping her heading into the wind
and holding position. I remember sitting on the pipe railing
watching the propeller coming up out of the water and spinning to beat hell and then submerging and just barley turning. The stern was rising and falling probably forty feet! If I
had fallen off I'd have gone through the prop and been
pureed shark meat, never to be seen again! I've often wondered if God had looked down and thought, "There's that
"dumb kid" again. If he ain't about to burn the match mill
down, he's on the stern of a ship in the ocean, sitting on the
railing, in the middle of a typhoon, watching the propeller
spin! I better get him back inside before he falls off!"

Chapter Five

Kadena Air Force Base, Okinawa

A couple of days later we disembarked on Okinawa. I think it was around August 9, 1956. Johnson said he saw a guy at the orderly room who was probably leaving on the Gaffee. He asked him, "How'd you like it over here?" The guy answered, "At first you won't like it, after awhile, you'll hate it."

Johnson by Squadron Emblem

After clearing in, as they called it, we learned that they didn't need anyone down on the flight line. So Johnson and I got assigned to the reclamation section. Here we are, the top two in our class, working in a damn junkyard! The tech sergeant in charge was Sergeant Caldwell. There was another sergeant working there also--Staff Sergeant Linderman. We called him Lindy. Lindy and his wife were really nice to us, and so were Sgt. Caldwell and his wife. They both had Johnson and me over to their houses several times for beer and hamburgers on the grill. They probably felt sorry for us misfits. When Sgt Caldwell introduced me as Airmen Hubbell to the twelve-fifteen Okinawans working there, they started laughing. He asked them what they were laughing at and they said, "Haboo! Haboo! Poisonous snake!" So that was my nickname from then on--Haboo!

The first thing Lindy did was to show us how to operate a twenty ton American crane! Then the one of us operating the crane would lift a five foot square by three feet high concrete block up about ten feet. The other guy would then

Johnson by "his 20 ton American crane".

slide a couple of F86 drop tanks under it. Then the guy operating the crane would release the brake and drop the concrete block and smash the drop tanks. We must have smashed a thousand of those drop tanks. And once in awhile we'd say, "Wonder what that kid that we thought was a "quart low" knew that we didn't know?" I've got to admit that it was kind of fun to operate that crane! Anything that needed lifting around the base, Johnson and I lifted it!

The most fun was to go off the flight line to the motor pool to get fuel. There was a guard shack at the exit point and the electrical wires going to the shack were about six inches lower than the boom. So you'd have to keep rolling until about two feet before the boom was going to hit the wires. Then you'd tap the air brakes and the boom would do a "curtsy" under the wires. Neither Johnson nor I ever "got" the wires but our replacement took them out the first time he tried it alone. I don't remember how many airplanes we lifted when they'd land gear up, or when the gears would collapse during a typhoon etc.

The base LOX (Liquid Oxygen) plant was out of service for about a month. So everyday a C119 would fly down from Japan with a 500 gallon tank of liquid oxygen aboard. My roommate, John Duede, ran the LOX plant so he'd call us when the "119" was arriving and Johnson and I'd go down and offload the full tank and position the empty to be winched back onto the "119" for the trip back to Japan.

One day I was doing the offloading. I had driven the crane up behind the "119" and swung the boom around between the two tail fins, later I learned they were, "vertical stabilizers". The 500 gallon "LOX" tank was about ten feet long and eight feet wide and weighed about 7,000lbs.

Which wasn't much for the old American "twenty ton" crane. Johnson and Duede grabbed the cable block, which probably weighed 150lbs itself, and wrestled it up inside the "119" and hooked it to a chain that was attached to the

"LOX" tank. I was, "booming off to the side" as we called it, and when I started putting some tension on the cable the crane would tilt a little to the load side. I was just putting enough tension on to start the "LOX" tank sliding out the back of the "119" and down the ramp, I got it down the ramp and was applying a little more tension to start lifting it up, when all of a sudden the chain

Looking into the LOX plant you can see two, 500gal ox tanks

broke. That released the side tilt of the crane and caused the cable block to spring back toward me!! My first thought was, "Oh shit, it's coming right back in my lap!! Fortunately for me the horizontal stabilizer on the "119" stopped it! Unfortunately for the "119" though it didn't stop it until it was halfway through it!! We hooked a tug to the "119" and towed it up to the "sheet metal shop" and in a few hours they had it repaired and sent it back to Japan. I blamed that on Johnson and Dude, for not properly inspecting, "their chain"! That cost them a couple of beers for me at the club after work, to "calm my nerves"!! (We always had a good excuse for why we had to drink and get, about half drunk!)

In fact, that night I was leaving the latrine and was walking back to my room and Johnson was coming down the hall, and he stopped and said, "You must be drunk!" I said,

"I am not, why do you say that?" He said, "Because I see two of you!" I figured they must be having one hell of a party in his room. I'd have joined them but I wanted to write a letter to my new wife.

Actually, working in the "junkyard" wasn't bad duty. We just couldn't figure out why the government would spend all that money to put us through mechanics school, see us graduate the top of our class, then ship us some place where they don't need us, and put us to work, in a "junkyard!"

We had cases of bayonets at the "junkyard," so we made a target with a red bulls-eye on a door out back. We'd spend hours throwing bayonets for a dollar or a beer a bulls-eye." At the end of the day it would pretty much average out.

One day Johnson found a motor scooter amongst the junk. We figured we could get it running. All it needed was a little welding and TLC we figured. One day we were on our knees on the dirt floor out in the shop welding on our "little pride and joy", when I heard this voice say, "What are you doing, airmen?" I looked up and saw this "Bird Colonel" looking down at us. I said, "We're making ourselves a motor scooter sir." He must have figured we were a couple of jackoffs, and any speech would be a waste of his time so he just walked away. Probably thinking, "Who the hell recruited those two jackoffs?" (Hmmm, that's what the "TI" had called us, could he have been right??)

We had been working in the junkyard about three months when Sgt. Caldwell came out and said we'd have to go take the "5" level test tomorrow. I said, "I thought you're supposed to work on airplanes for a year or so after school before you take the "5" level test. We haven't even worked on a airplane in the three months we've been here!" He said, "You'll probably flunk it but at least you'll know what it's like." So that evening, true to form, Johnson and I went down to the club and drank beer and I smoked cigarettes, and we got, about half drunk as usual.

The next morning, November 7, 1956, we reported to the theater, along with about a hundred other guys taking various tests. There were about maybe thirty guys taking the 43151B test-the "5" level test.

About a week later Sgt. Caldwell came out and said, "Hubbell, what would the Base Commander want to talk to you about?" I thought, "Oh shit, how does he know it was me that ran the guard gate on the motorcycle last week?!" Johnson had a BSA, "Road Rocket" motor cycle.

He'd had it bored out and that thing would "scream." Funny we never got killed on it. He and I had gone into the

Johnson on his BSA motorcycle

village, got about half drunk as usual, and I was driving back to the base. I got within thirty feet of the guard gate and for some stupid reason I decided, I didn't want to stop, and instead I dropped two gears and did a "wheelie" past the guards. I can still hear them hollering, "Halt, halt," but I figured, they ain't going to shoot a couple of young airmen in the back so I kept going. We parked the BSA over in the next squadron for a few days so we could report it stolen if the AP's picked it up. They didn't, and we'd just brought it back to our barracks the day before. I said to Johnson, "How the hell does he know it was me that ran the guard gate?"

I went in and picked up the phone and said, "This is Airmen Hubbell sir." The voice on the other end of the line said, "Airmen Hubbell, this is the Base Commander, and I'm calling you personally to congratulate you on your "5" level test." I said, "Was it that bad sir?" And he said, "You only got the highest score "ever" made in the Air Force, 145 out of 150 right." I thought, "Damn it, I'd have gotten them all right if I hadn't gotten, about half drunk the night before!"

He then asked if Airman Johnson was there. I said "He's outside about a seventy five feet away, shall I get him sir?" He said, "No, just tell him he got second highest with 135 right!" Then I found myself thinking, (Hmmm, maybe I'm only about the fiftieth dumbest kid in the world!!) The next week Johnson and I were put in charge of crews down at the maintenance hanger on the flight line. But Johnson didn't like being cooped up inside the hangar all day, so after a couple of weeks he went back down to the "junkyard" and got his old job back. (I think he had "fallen in love" with that old crane, and missed her.) He spent the rest of his time on Okinawa driving that crane, lifting this or that, and standing by with it out at the fire station near the runway when needed.

But about a month later Johnson and I found out we had still missed getting promoted to "Airman Second." Here we had gotten the highest and second highest scores at school,

PERSONNEL ACTION MEMORANDUM)
NUMBER   149)   19 December 1956

1. Announcement is made of category A (QUALIFIED) APT OF FNA,
ORG, test AFSC, Score and date tested IND. Appropriate entries w/b
made on AMN AF Form 7 IA'. AFM 35-12

RANK	NAME	AFSN	TEST AFSC	SCORE	DATE TESTED
	HQ, 18TH FITBOMWG, APO 239, PERAM #149, 19 Dec 56 (Cont)				
A/2C	Gulden, Donald	13527362	43151	115	6 Nov 56
A/2C	Hinkle, Dennis	14515631	43151	115	6 Nov 56
A/2C	Horne, Gary B	17450082	43151	115	6 Nov 56
A/3C	Hubbell, Leslie	17444822	43151	145	7 Nov 56
A/3C	Johnson, Melvin E	17450584	43151	135	7 Nov 56
A/2C	Koch, Donald M	17411942	43151	107	7 Nov 56
A/2C	Lovelett, Dennis R	16515511	43151	130	7 Nov 56
A/3C	McFarland, Charles R	16513356	43151	133	7 Nov 56
A/2C	Morch, Charles	12477599	43151	117	7 Nov 56
A/2C	Presol, John D Jr	17450153	43151	119	9 Nov 56
A/2C	Salcilo, Ruben	18430021	43151	91	9 Nov 56
A/2C	Snyder, Daniel W	16361923	43151	117	9 Nov 56
A/2C	Stewart, John,	14548705	43151	132	9 Nov 56
A/3C	Thoroughman, Jack R	25192698	43151	109	9 Nov 56
A/3C	Whitley, John L	15543323	43151	101	9 Nov 56
SSGT	Griggs, William	18398589	43171	130	6 Nov 56
SSGT	Gurganious, Robert J Jr	14380939	43171	128	6 Nov 56
SSGT	Italiano, Cosmo Jr	12379303	43171	109	7 Nov 56
SSGT	Laffler, Jack A	17374231	43171	109	7 Nov 56
A/3C	Mangos, Theonlin N	14569247	43250	128	6 Nov 56
A/2C	Smith, Watson S	14152265	43250	128	6 Nov 56
A/3C	Strand, Bruce E	16518565	43250	121	6 Nov 56
A/3C	Vaness, John W	16518523	43250	132	6 Nov 56
A/3C	Woodward, Vinnie L	19534512	43250	109	6 Nov 56
A/2C	Artz, Allen A	13542670	43251	103	6 Nov 56
A/3C	Blazier, Charles F	13537699	43251	90	6 Nov 56
A/3C	Brett, Harold	13599759	43251	108	6 Nov 56
A/3C	Brown, James W	14569950	43251	129	6 Nov 56
A/3C	Fowle, Raymond J	11302492	43251	97	6 Nov 56
A/2C	Kurtz, Mike L	13540296	43251	111	7 Nov 56
A/3C	Langevin, Alfred W	11304764	43251	102	7 Nov 56
A/3C	Muncie, Carl E	15543031	43231	106	7 Nov 56
A/2C	Blackburn, Phillip J	15535380	64151	102	7 Nov 56
A/2C	Scott, Wayne E	14520694	64151	102	7 Nov 56
A/2C	Thompson, William R	14523496	64151	102	7 Nov 56

and then we got the highest and second highest scores ever
made on the Five Level test and didn't even get promoted!
We were so depressed we went down to the club and got,
about half drunk!! (that's was as good an excuse as any we
figured!)

So I went and talked to Master Sergeant Blalock who was
my boss. He had been in the Bataan death march. He listened to me and sent me to Lieutenant Miku, who was the
maintenance officer. He sent me to the squadron adjutant,
who sent me to the squadron commander, who got me pro-

moted! (Johnson, wasn't a "squeaker," so he didn't get "greased") He made it the next promotion cycle though!

On March 20, 1957, early in morning, Lt. Miku called me over to his office. He told me that one of our F86s was lying, gear up, in the middle of the runway down at Tainan,

---

HEADQUARTERS
18TH FIGHTER BOMBER WING (FEAF)
APO 239, San Francisco, California

WAG   22 March 1957

SUBJECT: Letter Order #149

TO: Personnel Concerned

     A/2C LESLIE V HUBBELL, AF17444822, 18TH FLDMAINTRON, 18TH FITBOMWG, this STA, WP on or ABT 20 MAR 57 to Tainan, Formosa, on TDY for APPRX five (5) days, CIPAP, for the purpose of assisting in removal of crashed F-86-F A/C. (DPUO); and UCWR proper ORG this STA. Sixty-five (65) LBS BAG AUTH while TVL by air. IDENT TAGS w/b worn while TVL by air. MPC up to one hundred fifty (150) DOLS may be converted prior to DEPT. Funds in excess of one hundred fifty (150) DOLS w/b converted to DOL INST prior to DEPT, are CFM. ESPWO. TDN. TBMAA. OA#57-109 5773400 074-3210 P458-02 S62-321. AUTH: AFM 35-11.

     BY ORDER OF THE COMMANDER:

                                        Caesar A. Ricci

DISTRIBUTION: CAESAR A RICCI
  3-PER INDIV   1STLT, USAF
  3-EA ORGN CONC   AST ADJ
  3-KPC-A
  3-WPC-O
  3-KAC-F
  3-WPC-F
  1-KAC-A
  1-201 FILE
  5-WAG

Formosa. He said to take whoever and whatever I needed and get it all loaded on a C119 down on the flight line and get down there, ASAP and get that F86 off the runway! I "recruited" a couple of guys, (Johnson couldn't go because of being on standby duty on the flight line with the crane.)

We loaded a tug, a power cart, a hydraulic "mule," a compressor and some air bags, jacks, a tow bar and tool boxes on a C119 and I threw a change of clothes and shaving kit etc. in a bag we were off the ground and on the way within, 90 minutes!! They landed and taxied the C119 right up next to the F86 and lowered the ramps. The F86 was sitting about 500 feet from the end of the runway and right on the center-line! We rolled the compressor, power cart and "mule" off and hooked them up and started them up. We put four air bags under the F86 and by the time we had the hoses hooked up, the compressor was up to pressure. We inflated the bags lifting the F86 up, put some jacks under her, deflated the bags, and put the bags and compressor back in the C119. We lowered the gear, looked it over, cycled it a couple of times. It looked OK. The F86 had no serious damage. She just had some scraping marks so we lowered the jacks, put everything except the tug back in the C119 and towed her to the ramp – all in about another hour! There was also a pilot with us and he looked her over, and figured it was safe to fly. So he had some fuel put in, I hooked up the power cart, and he fired her up, taxied out and took off. He was probably landing back at Kadena, within thirty minutes!

The C119 pilots weren't in any hurry to get back so we decided to spend the night there. I remember going for a walk after supper. I had gotten off the base a little I think. I looked off to my left and there was a Chinese soldier (I think he was Chinese) standing up in the trees with a rifle that had a bayonet on it. He was looking at me with what I thought was considerable interest. I decided, "Maybe I better turn around and get back on the base."

The next morning they fired up the C119 and we flew back to Okinawa. I still remember looking out the window when we took off, and down at the land and ocean, looking at ships etc., and thinking, "God, this is beautiful, I wish I was smart enough to be a pilot." but I knew I wasn't. A couple of days after I got back, I got my orders to go!

On April 2, 1957, I got orders to attend "F100" school for about a month. From the "junkyard" to the "flight line" to Formosa, and now to F100 school in just a few months! I thought, "This is great for a "dumb kid" from Cloquet, Minnesota!" If I hadn't been so lonesome for my new wife back home I would have stayed there! Our Maintenance Officer was Lt. Miku. I remember when I went to talk to him about not getting pro-moted after get-ting the highest

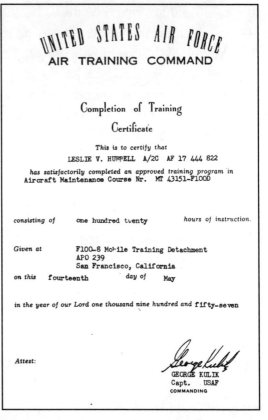

UNITED STATES AIR FORCE

AIR TRAINING COMMAND

Completion of Training
Certificate

This is to certify that
LESLIE V. HUPPELL A/2C AF 17 444 822

has satisfactorily completed an approved training program in
Aircraft Maintenance Course Nr. MT 43151-F100D

consisting of   one hundred twenty   hours of instruction.

Given at   F100-8 Mobile Training Detachment
                  APO 239
                  San Francisco, California
on this   fourteenth   day of   May

in the year of our Lord one thousand nine hundred and fifty-seven

Attest:
                                    George Kulik
                                  GEORGE KULIK
                                  Capt.   USAF
                                  COMMANDING

score ever made on the Five Level test and Johnson and I were first and second in our class at mechanics school, and they send us over here to work in a junkyard!. He had said, "Don't feel bad. I was going to dental school when I got drafted and they made me a "Maintenance Officer!" And, he said, "I don't know anything about airplanes and I don't care to learn anything about them either!" He just wanted to put his six years in and get out and go back to dental school, he said. So when we got orders to go to F100, school, he called me and asked if he could sit by me and if I would help him pass the course. Of course I would, and I did!

(He put a nice letter of appreciation in my file before I left Okinawa.)

AERO REPAIR BRANCH
18th Field Maintenance Squadron
18th Fighter Bomber Wing
APO 239 San Francisco, California

8 January 1958

SUBJECT: Performance of A/2c Leslie V. Hubbell, AF17444822

TO: Whom it May Concern

    1. Airman Second Class Leslie V. Hubbell, AF17444822, has been in my Aero Repair Branch in the Aircraft Maintenance Hanger for his entire overseas tour. During this period, Airman Hubbell has been an outstanding worker in his shop. He has preformed his job well under all conditions.

    2. This letter could go on and list all his qualities and not mean anything, but to us, who have had him under us, we would like to thank him for a job well done, for a job and an attitude that has reflexed his honest desire to do his very best.

    3. We hope that his next station and tour will be a satisfactory one and fully recommend him to his next commander.

ALEXANDER M. MIKU
1st Lt, USAF
OIC, Aero Repair Branch

One day in early to mid May I was working down in the maintenance hangar and I heard this horrible squealing and screeching going on out on the flight line.

I walked around the corner of the hangar to see what the hell was making all the noise. Coming down the taxi-way was a C124!! Johnson and I had gone to school on one of those at Sheppard Air Force Base! It was so big it looked like a whole city block coming!! I had never seen one taxing before so I didn't know the brakes made so much noise! It tuned out it was going to be on display for Armed Forces Day. It was fun to go through one again! And of course we made sure we were around when it taxied back out and took off!!

The flight line taken by Duede from the LOX plant

A C124

One day my crew and I had finished up an engine change on an F100. It needed a wash job, so I hooked it onto a tug and towed it down to the wash rack. I got it down there at about 11:30, and the kid running the wash rack was hosing down an F86 that he was just finishing up.

He was a Chinese kid. Everybody thought he must know Judo and Karate. I was so dumb when I first got to Okinawa, that I thought Judo and Karate must be a couple other Chinese kids! I found out later that Judo and Karate were what we called fighting back on the farm. That kid was always "judo chopping" something. I told him the F100 needed a wash job and it was going to be flying at 1500 (3 P.M.) and I'd be back to get it at 1400 (2 P.M.) He said he didn't have time to do it and I said, "Find time to do it!" One thing led to another and we ended up in a heated discussion about getting this F100 washed.

Next thing I know he's running toward me. When he was about six feet from me, I squatted down, rolled on my back, and hit him with both feet, right in the stomach, sending him about six feet in the air and probably twelve feet beyond me. By the time he hit the concrete and was getting up I was already there and put a hammer lock around his neck, reached around and grabbed his legs and jumped, throwing us both into the air. I came down on his stomach, knocking the wind out of him! I got up and was going to stomp him, but he'd had enough. I told him, "I'll be back at 1400 to get the F100." I thought, as I drove away, "He might know "judo and karate," but he sure don't know "farm fighting" When I went back down to get the F100, it was done. I could see he was bruised and still hurting, so I apologized. We shook hands and ended up becoming pretty good friends.

I was a skinny little kid when I was growing up so it seemed like someone was always picking a fight with me! I remember what happened one day when we lived in Scanlon, which joins Cloquet on the southeast side. I was walking home from school. We only lived a block from the school. I'd guess I was in the third or forth grade. I couldn't have been any older because I started fifth grade at the Leech School after we moved out to the farm eight miles west of town. Anyway, a kid by the name of Russell lived a block up the road from my house. He and I got into a fight and he beat me up. I was hurting and went into the back porch. Some of my mother's relatives from Remer were at the house visiting. One of my uncles saw me in the porch and came out and asked me what happened. I told him, "That kid out there," (pointing at Russell) "beat me up!" He took me by the hand and led me out to where Russell was. He said, "That kid?" I said, "Yes." I thought he was going to beat Russell up!! Instead, he said to me, "You can beat him up!" So Russell and I got into it again, and I got beat up again! I thought, "My uncle must be dumber than me. At least I knew the first time I was beat!" It was probably just a few days later that Russell and I had gone down the Scanlon hill to the railroad tracks--just fooling around. We had found some choke cherries so we filled our pockets and had our hands full. We were coming back up the hill and were just about to turn right, up the alley, when a car came down the hill with the driver's window open. That was too much of a temptation for Russell, so he threw a handful of choke cherries at it! Not to be outdone, I let go with a handful of choke cherries too! That guy hit the brakes, tires were squealing, gears were grinding into reverse, and Russell and I were running, up the alley!

Russell was heading home and I was on the back porch steps of my house, when the guy came up the alley! As soon as I got in the porch, I saw my mother, with her back to me, mopping the kitchen floor. I closed the screen door with out making a sound, then I went in and, very quietly, stepped in and stood behind the open kitchen door. It was just a few seconds before the guy was on the back porch, madder than hell, hollering at my mother! "Where is the kid that just ran in here? He threw berries at my car!" My mother said, "No kid just came in here." He said, "I saw him!" She said, "I've been right here mopping the floor and no kid has come in here, so beat it! The guy said, "That's why these kids are the way they are today, they get no discipline!! I'll go find that other kid, then!" My mother went back to mopping the floor, still with her back to me, so I very quietly stepped around the door, backed into the porch, out the screen door, closed it without a sound, and was gone! I looked around for a while but didn't see the guy's car around Russell's house or anyplace, so I went up and knocked on the door to see if Russell was home. He was, and we stayed out of trouble and fights for the rest of the day even!

I also remember a few months later we were out of school for recess. It was a nice warm winter day. Russell was up the steps on the porch, about ten feet above the playground. The school was a big, one room building. There was a library and the different classes were, in small groups, here and there.

Ms Penrose was the principal and probably a teacher too. Russell threw a snowball down and hit me. So of course, I made a snowball, and threw it back at him! Just as I let it go, the big double doors of the school opened, and Ms. Penrose walked out on the porch to announce, "Recess is over." My snowball just missed her, going over her shoulder into the library and splattering all over the library floor! I can still see her. She looked ten feet tall and was giving me the "come here" with her curled up finger! Since I was the only kid standing out front, she had me, "dead to rights!" I ended up sweeping up the library floor and sitting in the corner for thirty minutes! And if I ever find out where that damn Russell Fjeld lives now; I'm going to have a beer with him, and we'll arm wrestle to see who pays!!"

When we moved out to the farm we had four cows. Two of them were easy to milk; the other two were hard to milk. So my older brother, who outweighed me by about twenty pounds, and I would fight over who was going to milk the easy cows. I would always lose. But one day we got into it, on the path between the house and the barn, and for the first time I was on top and it was pay back time! My dad saw us and tried to pull me off, but I wasn't about to let go yet, so he went and got a two by four and broke it over my back before I'd quit.

It wasn't but a few days later and my younger brother and I both wanted to go partridge hunting. The only problem was, it was my shotgun, and his belt full of shotgun shells. He outweighed me by about fifteen pounds too, I'd guess. We were upstairs in the boys' room and, after a little scuffling, I had him by the neck and the seat of his pants and up over my head! It's a good thing my dad was home and heard us, because he came running up the stairs, about the time I was probably going to throw my brother, down the stairs!

So there I was, bare-chested with my younger brother over my head. My dad grabbed that belt full of shotgun shells off the bed, and swung it across my bare chest. I dropped my brother, "gently", onto his bed and had shotgun shell marks embedded in my chest for about ten days! My Dad said, "Damn it Les, can't you ever go more than three days without getting into a fight with somebody?!" I said, "I don't start em dad, I just finish em!"

One time I asked him why we had moved out of town to the farm. He said, "to keep you boys out of trouble." Heck, that didn't work! I came home from school one day, about a month later; changed clothes and went down to clean the barn. When I got down there, Dad said, "The FBI was here looking for you today." I said, "The FBI!" What did they want!? He said, "Somebody blew up Kotiranta's mailbox, but I told them, "my boys wouldn't do that." (Kotiranta was a county commissioner, and they lived on the next farm west of us.) "Nope, wasn't me dad!" (I knew some kids who had some "cherry bombs" though and had probably done it!)

My dad use to tell me, every now and then, that I was a "scrapper of a kid" not long after I was out of diapers even! He said when he'd scold me I'd look at him like I was going to "spit in his eye!" He told me that, when we lived out north of Cloquet where I was born and I hadn't even started school yet, when he'd scold me, I'd go out and knock his car out of gear, jump out, and let it roll back down the hill, into the "pickers." He said, "I sure got tired of walking through them thistles to get my car!" (I don't remember my mother or dad ever spanking me, they probably should have though!)

I can actually remember, when I was still in diapers, being down at the creek, about 150 feet north of the house. There was a board across the creek, and the other kids were already on the other side in the woods. I was halfway across on the board, when I heard my mother hollering at me. I looked back and she was running down the path to get me. I got scared and jumped in the creek to get away! Luckily it was only about six inches deep, and 4 feet wide, but I can still today remember her stepping into the creek and grabbing me by the arm and my now soaking wet diapers and picking me up out of the creek!

Back to Okinawa...I remember one Sunday morning after breakfast, (hmmm, we must not have gotten about half drunk the night before because we wouldn't have gotten up for breakfast if we had) Johnson said, "Let's take the BSA for a ride up north as far as we can." So we loaded up and headed out. We rode north for a couple hours or more, kind of exploring this road or that. We rode down one trail, and pretty soon we got to the end of it and we could see a runway, a few buildings and a black airplane with a guard around it. We were up kind of high in the woods and looking down at this airplane wondering what would just one airplane be doing here, and why is it all black, why is there a guard there? (I'm not sure if it even had markings on it.) We figured, maybe we shouldn't be there, so we turned around and left. We got back to the main road, which is about like one of our alleys, and Johnson said, "Your turn" so I drove on the way back.

We got to the base just before the chow hall was due to open and there was a line of about fifty guys waiting. We come tooling into the parking lot, really cool like. I laid that BSA over on her right side, making a nice curving approach to where I wanted to park it. We hit some sand and slid along for about twenty feet scraping the case guards, hit a bare spot, the BSA popped back up straight, right where I was going to park her anyway. I put the kick stand down, and Johnson and I got off to a standing ovation! And, of course we acted like "we do that all the time!"

I remember back in "basic training" in Texas, the "TI" would have us fallout on the street in the morning for role call. He'd holler out, "Hubbell, Leslie V." Occasionally someone would ask me, "What's the "V" stand for Hubbell? I'd say, "The "V" is for "virgin for short, but not for long!"

Duede had his friends that he worked and partied with, and most everything I did was with Johnson, but Duede and I had some great talks and shared a few beers now and then.

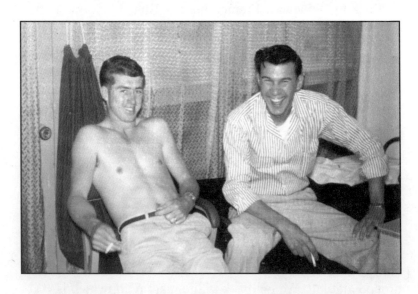

Hubbell and Duede. Probably the only picture taken of Hubbell, on Okinawa when he wasn't, about half drunk!

One thing great about Duede though, was when I'd come back from the village or club, about half drunk, he'd always make sure I had a paper bag to throw up in so I wouldn't make a mess all over the floor. It was good, I thought, to have a roommate who was neat.

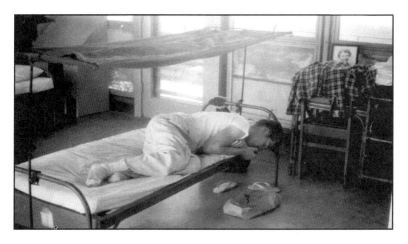

Hubbell, about half drunk, and maybe a little more!

One morning though, after Johnson and I had done our share to support the club again, (Johnson always figured it was our duty to drink enough so the club wouldn't go broke) I awoke to find my bed soaking wet and full of broken glass. My wall locker and Duede's were lying on the floor. My first thought was, "I've got to talk to Duede about some of these parties he has!" Back then I didn't just sleep, I died! Duede and his friends would come back from the club, feeling no pain, and want me to wake up and talk but I was fast asleep. He'd tell me the next morning that they'd have me bouncing a foot and a half in the air over my bunk and I'd just snort and keep sleeping. It got to be that they judged how severe a typhoon was by whether it woke me up or not!

I remember when I was maybe fourteen years old, back on the farm, my dad had come home from work about midnight. I heard him holler up the stairs, "Get up boys, the cows are out on the highway!" I got up and was hooking up my bibs (overalls) when I thought, "Why am I doing this?" I took my bibs off, shut the lights off, and went back to sleep. The next morning at breakfast, Dad, said, "What's the matter with you, too good to get up and help get the cows off the highway?" I said, "Oh, is that what you were doing?"

It turned out that a typhoon had hit the island after I had gone to sleep. (A typhoon, in case you don't know it, is the same thing as a hurricane over here, but over there it has a slanted eye.) When a typhoon would hit the island, we were confined to the barracks for about three days until it blew by. We only had C rations to eat. You didn't want to be outside! The winds could easily hit 100 plus miles per hour and you could get your head cut off from a piece of corrugated metal from the roof of a hut in the village or a truck hood or a piece of metal off an airplane or a two x four doing 100 mph!

We'd build a little campfire on the tile floor in the common area where the wings of the barracks came together, to heat our soup or whatever we were getting ready to eat. The

Our barracks, taken by Duede from the LOX plant)

barracks were made of poured concrete, walls, floors every-thing, with windows which were practically from floor to ceiling tall, so we figured we wouldn't burn the place down.

Whoever was doing the building maintenance must have been really nice guys because we never got our asses chewed out for doing that! They'd just replace a few tiles after every typhoon. Thinking about it now, I wonder why we didn't put the cover off a garbage can on the floor first to build our fire in?? (Hmmm, have I grown a little smarter with age?)

We probably rode out, as we called it, two or three typhoons while we were over there. I remember we had five or six "gooney birds" (DC3's) tied down along the taxiway and a typhoon was approaching. We had filled them with fuel, chained them down and put sandbags about a foot apart along the spar on top of the wing to breakup the airflow. After the typhoon blew by, we went down to inspect for damage. Four of the gooney birds had danced around so much that their left gears had collapsed and they were down on their left wing tips! Johnson was busy for a couple of weeks after that with the crane lifting, not only those gooney birds, but a lot of other things and putting them back in place. We got where we liked typhoons. It was like being on vacation and camping out, and getting, about half drunk!

I only got up once in the 18 months I was on Okinawa to go to "early chow" at 3:30am. I just couldn't sleep so thought I might as well get up and go have breakfast. There were about 50 guys in line, I was about in the middle when I looked back, and about 15 guys behind me, I saw a Indian kid. I thought, "that sure looks like "Skip Pellerin" from Cloquet." "Skip" was one year ahead of me in high school, and lived about 5 miles from the farm I lived on. I thought, it can't be him, halfway around the world at 3:30 in the morning. I looked back again and thought, no, all those Indian kids look the same, it can't be him. I turned around and was talking to some guys ahead of me but kept wondering, "is that Skip or not." Finally, I turned back around and said, "Skip" and he looked over and said, Hubbell??. What a small world we said, two kids from Cloquet, Minnesota meeting at 3:30 in the morning on Okinawa, half way around the world from home! Skip had flown down from Japan the afternoon before and was going back after breakfast. That was the only morning I had gotten up to go the "early chow" and that was the only time "Skip" had come to Okinawa. What's the chance of that happening, we wondered.

When our eighteen months were up on Okinawa, Johnson and I got orders to go to Bolling Air Force Base, Washington, DC. Boy, did we get, ribbed by our friends! "You guys better shape up because you're going to be right under the nose of the Pentagon! You better starch your fatigues, get a haircut, polish your boots, learn to salute right, and quit drinking!" (authors note: just for old times sake, I wrote everything about Okinawa while I was, "about half drunk!")

Chapter Six

Going to Washington, DC

Once again we got a thirty day leave before we had to report to Bolling Air Force Base, Washington, DC.

We lived with the wife's parents at the store until we left for DC. That was OK except we had to wait to make love until they would go out into the store about 8:30 in the morning, or I'd have kept them awake all night!! Besides, I didn't want them to know that I was "violating their daughter." But I suppose they already knew that when she had a baby girl nine months after I had left for Okinawa!

Through our letters back and forth from Cloquet and Okinawa, we had agreed we should buy a trailer house and pull it out to Bolling AFB. The wife, with the help of her Dad, had bought a 1947 eight foot wide by thirty foot long Alma trailer house and a 1952 Oldsmobile Super 88 to pull it with. By the time I got home the father-in-law had an easy hitch already installed on the Olds – all wired up and ready to go! I suppose he knew I be more interested in his daughter, than trailer hitches, so he might as well get it done!

We left about ten days before I was supposed to report in at Bolling so we'd have plenty of time to get there and get the trailer house set up in the trailer park. It was 20 below zero the morning we were leaving! When I walked around the car and trailer house, checking things, I reached up and shook the back door handle on the trailer to make sure it was locked. It was so cold that it broke off right in my hand!

We headed out and made Chicago that evening. I had called my Uncle Willie in Chicago and he had given me directions to his house where we parked for the night. His wife had made a nice supper for us and we had a nice visit. The next morning Willie led me out to the freeway and we headed East on "I 80." We stayed on that for a couple of days until it turned into "I 76" just west of Youngstown, Ohio. When we got into Pennsylvania, it was called the "Pennsy Turnpike." Somehow we made it out to the Breezwood exit where "I 70" headed southeast down to Washington, DC. We found a motel off the freeway a mile or so. I had learned not to stay at a motel right on the freeway because I'd be awake all night listening to the trucks shifting gears and the tires whining!

The next morning when I checked out of the motel I asked the guy how to get back on "I 70" and he said, "Go down here a mile or so, take a right, go a half mile, turn left, etc., and it'll take you right out to the freeway.

Well, I must have taken a left when I should have taken a right because pretty soon were heading east on a narrow little state road 30. I was looking for a place to turn around but it was so narrow and winding that I couldn't find a place. Pretty soon were heading down a hill, winding left and right around corners, the trailer brakes were electric and getting hot and fading out! It wasn't long and I had no trailer brakes and the trailer was trying to pass the car up! The car brakes were "fading too! The car tires were squealing very loudly as the trailer kept trying to pass the car! I was swerving from the left side of that narrow road to the right side trying to stay ahead of the trailer all the time praying, that a car wouldn't be coming up the hill around the next corner!! I could hear the trailer tires squealing, the wife was screaming, and the baby was crying, and I was "scared shitless" and sure we were going to go off the road and down the hill into the trees and we were all going to die! (God had to have looked down and thought, "There's that dumb kid again. He ain't never pulled anything bigger than a hay wagon with a

Farmall tractor doing five miles an hour! And there he is, with a thirty foot trailer house pushing him 60 miles an hour, out of control and about ready to go off the road and down into the trees! He must think I've got nothing else to do but take care of him! If it wasn't for having his wife and baby with him, I'd teach him a lesson. But maybe he's scared himself enough this time that he might smarten up a little!")

Around the next corner, the road straightened out and started up a little grade. Now the car was pulling the trailer again and I got it under control and slowed down. I still couldn't find a place to pull over so when I got to a level, straight stretch of road, I just brought it to a stop right in the middle of the road. I hugged and kissed my wife and little ten-month-old daughter and we were all crying, glad to be alive. I went back to the trailer to check for damage. The furniture was thrown all about, the fan had come right out of the furnace, boxes we had packed and had sitting on the floor were ruptured from being bounced from wall to wall and their contents had spread all over the floor. I didn't care; we were alive. I checked the map. We had to turn around and go back because there was no other way to get to the freeway from where we were.

A couple of more miles down the road we went underneath an overpass. I noticed there was level ground for about twenty five feet back under it before it got to the bridge abutment on my side of the road. I backed the trailer up and jackknifed it under the bridge. There wasn't enough room to pull ahead and straighten out so I had to get out and unhook the car from the trailer. Then I had to go downhill, turn the car around, come back uphill, back up to the trailer, and get hooked up again. My wife was asking me what I was doing, but I didn't have time to answer her. I had to get this done before a semi or something came roaring down the hill and maybe couldn't stop either! We found our way back to "I 70" and I pulled into the first motel I could find. We'd had enough for one day!!

The next day we made it on down to Washington DC and pulled into Bolling Air Force Base. I pulled up to the guard gate and asked the guard how to get to the trailer park. He asked, "Do you have a reservation?" I said no. He said, "There's a two year waiting list, you're going to have to find someplace else, off base, to park it." I asked, "Do you know of anyplace I can park it until I find something?" He recommended Haines Point and gave me directions to get there. It was almost right downtown! When I checked in they told me I could only stay there for two weeks. I got the trailer hooked up to electricity, sewer and water and put a few blocks under it--blocks that the guy running the park was loaning me. We were glad to be there. It was late January and maybe fifty degrees above zero and there was no snow on the ground.

We got things straightened around inside enough that we could get to our bed and the baby's crib. Then we drove someplace and got something to eat. When we got back we took a little walk among the cherry trees. It was a nice warm evening. We turned in early; we were beat. The next morning we woke up about 7:30 and I looked out the window. I couldn't believe it! The ground was covered with snow, and a lot of it! There was at least a foot or more! I had the only vehicle in the park with snow tires on and we needed some groceries so I had to go to a store someplace. I went around to the other nearby campers parked there and asked if anyone else had to go get groceries. Three more people rode with me, and the Olds plowed right through the snow with that load in it! Within three days the snow had melted and the ground dried up again!

I got clearance onto the base and explained my situation and the sergeant told me, "Take whatever time you need to get your family settled, Airman Hubbell." That was nice of him I thought. I went to all the local trailer parks and they were full with waiting lists too. Someone had told me about a trailer park about fifteen miles south down the Indian Head Highway that might have a space. So the next day, as I was driving down there and was about five miles south of the base, I saw a trailer sitting in somebody's back yard. I figured, "If they have one, maybe they've got room for another one! So I took the next right and found my way back there. I knocked on the door and a guy opened it, I said, "Sir,"(I can be really polite when I'm desperate) I noticed driving down the highway that you have a trailer parked over there. Is there any chance you have room for another one?" He said, "No" but that one was my mother's and she died a couple of months ago so I could move it and put yours in there, if it isn't too big." I told him mine was eight by thirty, which was exactly what his mother's was! "How much?" I asked and he said, "Fifty bucks a month if you'll help me move my mother's trailer out of there." This was cheap according to what they were charging closer to the base so I grabbed it! The next day I went down and helped him, and the following day I hooked mine up to the Olds and pulled it down there. He let me use the blocks, shimming, and sewer and water line that had been under his mother's house and everything fit perfectly! (I thought, God must be looking down at me again, I thanked him!) Plus we were right under a big tree, in the shade, which was nice because we didn't have air conditioning. (A few months later though we got a "widow unit" because it was getting hot and really humid. I remember leaving the house, with newly starched and pressed fatigues or uniform on, and by the time I walked 20 feet to my car, I was almost soaking wet!)

Chapter Seven

Bolling Air Force Base
Washington, DC.

When I reported for duty, I was assigned to transit alert. Johnson was living on the base in the barracks so he'd been at transit alert and was already out on the flight line! My wife's parents had flown down within the week to help their daughter get the trailer organized and to see their granddaughter. (I'm sure they were so happy they were still alive that they better come see them before something else happens!)

When I'd leave the trailer about 3:30 in the afternoon to go to work, I'd tell them, "I'll be back about 4:30." I'd go to the base and about six guys would show up, we'd draw straws and two guys would stay and four would go home. I never worked a night while my wife's parents were visiting for a week! (That's what you call "the luck of the Irish!")

When they left I started pulling duty and one night about two weeks later I asked the "old" sergeant, who was probably forty years old then, "Sarge, how come I'm still here and six or seven guys have come and gone? I thought we were supposed to rotate in and out of here?" He said, "I like you, I want to keep you here." I put my arm on his shoulder and said, "Sarge, I like you too, but I didn't go to school to park and refuel airplanes. I want to get out on the flightline and maybe be a crew chief on a "B25" or something. He must have made a phone call because the next evening he said, "see that Tech Sergeant sitting on that tug out there, he wants to talk to you." I went out and introduced my self to Tech Sergeant, Delroy Mills. Turned out he was from

Durant, Oklahoma. He said, with his Okie drawl, "Sarge says, you're a pretty good head, and I've got three airplanes parked across the field by the Potomac River, that we crew for the Vice Chief of Staff's Office and I need someone for changing oil, polishing, changing plugs etc." I asked, "Any chance of getting on flying status?" He said, "None whatsoever, in fact you're two stripes short anyway. You need to be at least a staff sergeant to be a flight engineer on these airplanes." He said if I wanted to get on flying status I should stay where I was and I'd probably get on a B25. "But they are phasing those out and replacing them with U3's,"(Cessna 310"s) he added. "But," he said, "you would be immune from pulling any other duty on the base. And, we're a small outfit, so we don't have any 'yes sir, no sir,' just remember I'm the boss." He said, "In fact our area is guarded twenty four hours a day and nobody gets near these airplanes unless they have a top secret clearance." Well, the part about being immune from having to do any other duty on the base appealed to me so I took that job.

There were six flight engineers: Tech Sergeant Delroy Mills; Staff Sergeants Bruce Currie, Rex Young, Joe Dungan, Louie Ajjan, Rhuel Sperry; and a flight steward, Airmen Second Class Frank Dalhman.

We were parked on the west, side of Bolling AFB, right next to the Potomac River. We had a 35 foot dark blue, gooseneck semi-trailer for our office and three hard stands to park the airplanes on and a couple of open air engine covers to do our work in. We also had a tug, a power cart and some support equipment There was no electricity over there so we had a generator out back of the office. It could be cold right next to the river or it could be raining in the early morning, and I was usually the first one there so I'd end up freezing my "ass off" or soaked getting the generator fired up. After about a month of that shit I went over to base supply and got about fifty feet of wiring and a spring loaded

Office and engine stands. you can see the generator behind the office

switch and box and wired that generator so we could start it
and shut it off from inside the office! That was referred to as
the "Hubbell Switch" after that!

I worked at a Texaco station in the evenings and weekends
a few blocks from the trailer, on the Indian Head Hwy and
Livingston
Road, pump-
ing gas, wash-
ing wind-
shields and
doing oil
changes, etc.,
to make ends
meet.

Whenever
any one of the
those three
Convairs was
going to be

The old Texaco station had just one service bay with a hoist
for changing oil, a couple of gas pumps and a little office.
That got replaced with this brand new Texaco station with a
convenience store and eight fuel pumps several years back.

started, I'd be there asking, "Can I start it, can I start it, can I start it?" The flight engineers would always let me. After I learned to start them, then I'd say, "Can I taxi it, can I taxi it, can I taxi it?" So it wasn't long and if they had to go over to the other side of the base to pick up passengers I'd be there, "Can I start it, can I taxi it? Can I start it, can I taxi it?" And, they'd let me!

Those guys probably got to feeling like my Dad did when I was a junior in school. Years later he told me he almost hated to come home from work because all he'd hear from me was, "Can I get a car Dad, can I get a car Dad, can I get a car Dad?" One day he came home from work and before I could say anything, he said he had found a car for me! A guy he worked with down at the Paper Mill had a 1936 Cadillac for sale for $100.00. Luckily I had saved enough to buy it!

I'll never forget the first time I saw one of those Convairs pull into the hard stand, turn around, taxi back out, and then back up into the same hard stand! I couldn't wait to do that!

I had worked there only about three months and one day DelRoy said, "Hubbell, everybody on the base has to take a test in their job description." I said, "I'll take a f---off test." He said the only thing we can call you is a flight engineer." I said, "I ain't no flight engineer, I can't pass a flight engineer's test!" He said, "Well, that's the only thing we got to give you, so you'll have to take it." The next day we all went over to the other side of the base someplace and took the test. About ten days later I came to work one morning and DelRoy was sitting on the floor, in the doorway of the office, with his feet out on the steps. When I came walking over from the car, and was about twenty feet away, he said, "Hubbell, you son-of-a- bitch," in that Oklahoma drawl he had. And I said, "What's the matter Sarge, the wife kicked you out of bed last night and now your taking it out on me or what??" He said, " Who do the f--k do you think got the highest score on the flight engineers test?" I said, "I suppose you did, you're the boss, you've been flying these things for seven years, and been to factory schools. I suppose Currie got second, Rex third, Sperry fourth, Ajan fifth, Dungan sixth and I suppose I flunked the "son-of-a-bitch!"

He said, "you asshole, you got the highest score! How do you think that makes us look to the Colonel over in the Pentagon?" I said, "It probably makes it look like you guys should play a little less poker and study the tech orders a lot more!" (I was taking tech orders home and reading them at night. I don't have that great of a memory, but I must have been able to at least recognize a right answer!) So DelRoy made me a flight engineer as an airmen second! (That meant I'd be getting an extra $75 dollars a month flight pay so I could quit my night and weekend job at the Texaco station!)

Delroy took me with him on a couple of trips to Petersen Air Force Base, Colorado Springs, CO. And then he sent me off alone with a first lieutenant and Captain Hazelbaker, who was our co-pilot for the Vice Chief of Staff's Office. I suppose the purpose was to see if we'd make it back alive or not! I don't know how this young first lieutenant got to fly one of these airplanes. I figured he must have been the general's son-in-law, or he'd caught someone sleeping with someone they weren't supposed to be sleeping with, because he sure couldn't land that airplane! That Convair was my "pride and joy" and he was bouncing her on the runway, bad! But, we made it back with all the parts still on it and that lieutenant never came back, which was fine with me!

I'll never forget my first solo flight as a flight engineer, for the Vice Chief of Staff's Office on Air Force Convair #1. The Chief of Staff, General White, was going to Petersen AFB, Colorado Springs!

General White and his family had boarded the yacht, at a marina up near the Pentagon, and cruised down the Potomac River, to a dock about 150 yards south of where we were

Air Force Convair #1

located. There was a limousine waiting at the dock to bring
them to the airplane. He had his wife and daughters with
him on this trip. He stopped and talked with Delroy, who
was standing "fire guard," and then came up into the airplane, and introduced his wife and daughters to the flight
crew, and said, "You gentlemen can start up and leave whenever you're ready." He and his family went back and sat
down. He was a fine gentleman and I was as proud as I
could be, to be a flight engineer, for "The Vice Chief of
Staff's Office, with him and his family aboard! Our Convair
had a full galley and after about three hours into the flight
Frank served a fine steak dinner to everyone on board, even
me! I thought, "Life was great, for a dumb kid off the
farm!" (And, I thought, "Maybe I'm only the 100th dumbest kid in the world!") The flight was uneventful and
smooth, which is what you wanted when the General was
onboard.

One of the things you had to do, was to make damn sure
you didn't let an engine or two quit on the runway after
landing in Colorado Springs! Our engines were "idle adjusted"
for sea level in Washington DC, and Colorado Springs is
about 6100 feet higher so you had to have the mixture con-

trols right back almost into "idle cutoff" or they could flood out and quit! And of course you could lean them out too much and kill them too! You were always about two clicks away from either killing them or flooding them. I dreaded the thought of sitting out on the runway with both engines dead. If you lost one, it wouldn't be quite as bad because at least you could still taxi being it had hydraulic nose wheel steering. I was lucky; I never lost one, and I never heard that any of the other guys had either.

We'd stay where the General stayed, at the Antlers Hotel, in Colorado Springs, in case he got a call and had to return to DC, immediately! We were there for a couple of days and had an equally uneventful flight back to DC. The Convair was "super charged, pressurized and air conditioned" so we'd always be up between fourteen and eighteen thousand feet. Frank prepared and served another fine meal to all aboard on the way home. "Life was good for a 'dumb kid' just off the farm!"

When General LeMay would go to Colorado Springs it was a whole different story though! He was always alone, at least on my flights as I remember. (Hmmm, maybe he didn't trust me with his family yet.) He'd of course, come down the Potomac on the yacht too. When the yacht passed our hard stand, I'd start up number two, aka the right engine. When the tower would see that engine start up, they'd shut down the whole airport, "nothing moved", except Air Force Convair # 1.

When LeMay was coming up the steps, Frank would give me a nod and I'd crank number one right along side him and pray I'd get it started before he got to the top of the steps! (I always did, but dreaded what might happen if I didn't! LeMay was known for not having much patience, with anyone!) Then I'd have to get up and squeeze into the radio rack, and LeMay would throw his hat on the hat shelf and squeeze past me and get into the pilot's seat.

He would never say anything to me, not even to Captain Hazelbaker! He'd just sit there and chomp on his cigar! Captain Hazelbaker would release the brakes and we'd start taxiing toward the runway. He'd ride the brakes so I could do my run up checks along the way and we didn't stop for anything. When we got to the runway, we'd just turn onto it, I'd go to takeoff power and we'd take off.

It was about an six hour flight to Colorado Springs as I remember. On one flight we were about two hours out and LeMay said to me, "We're five minutes late." So I bumped the manifold pressures up about three inches and an hour later he gave me a "OK", so I backed off a couple of inches. I always kidded the other guys that I was "LeMay's favorite" because I was the only one he ever talked to!

I remember one night we were taking some foreign dignitaries, some "Prince" of someplace and his aides up to New York City, probably La Guardia Airport. The cabin door was open. I just happened to look back and saw one of the aides reading a Playboy magazine in the front row as the Prince was coming up the aisle. The Prince saw that and grabbed the magazine and hit the aide over the head with it, threw it on the floor, and stormed toward the back of the airplane! That was worth a laugh, but I bet that poor aide became a "camel jockey" when they got back home!

It was late, past midnight, by the time we got back from New York. I had come out early the next morning to get Number "1" re-fueled. I cleaned the windshields, added oil, wiped the oil off the nacelles and gear doors and looked her over. Frank got the cabin cleaned up and restocked with supplies and ready to go. Then I stood "fire guard" for all three airplanes and they departed again.

They were all going to be gone for a few days and the non-flying engineers were taking a couple days off to "catch up at home." So I had the place all to myself!! I was in charge even!! Of course, there wasn't much left to be in charge of, just me and the generator, I guess! About, 9:30 I'm was in the office, having a cup of coffee and filling out my per diem form for yesterday's flight when all of a sudden, there's a master sergeant, from the other side of the base in the doorway, chewing my ass!

"How come you're not over on the other side helping with the base cleanup? What the hell makes you think you're too good to do be doing that, Airman Hubbell!!??"

We had a direct line to Colonel Steffe's office over in the pentagon He was the "Aide-de-Camp" to General White, and our boss. I picked up the phone and luckily the Colonel answered. I said, "Colonel Steffes, this is Airman Hubbell." He said, "Yes, Les, how was your flight to New York last night and what can I help you with?" I told him the flight had gone well, and we had gotten back about 12:30 last night and I was out here at 6:00 this morning to see all three airplanes off again. But, I said, "I have a Sergeant "So and So," as I read his name and serial number off of his fatigues, "standing in the doorway here, chewing my ass because I'm not over on the other side cleaning up the base." I said, "Should I be doing that, sir?"

He said, "Hand him the phone Les," and I did. I could hear him chewing this sergeant's ass and telling him to "get the hell off our area and give the phone back to me." That sergeant handed me the phone, and turned around and all but ran off the area.

Colonel Steffes said, "Did that take care of it, Les?" I said, "Yes sir, there was nothing but dust behind him as he left." He said, "I told him if he ever comes back over there I will have his ass court-martialed." It turned out Delroy and this sergeant didn't get along too well and he must have figured with Delroy out of town, he could put me to work. He didn't know though, that I figured "Manual Labor" was some guy living down in Mexico!

One time we had two airplanes going out to the Springs.

I was on our number "1" and Ajan was on number "2". About 8:30 pm., Ajan and I walked down to our favorite little country bar, about a half mile from the Antlers, and had a few beers and listened to a really good country band and singer that they always had there.

We were walking back about 12:30 and passing by a movie theater when the door started rattling. I looked over and there was a woman inside. I went over and asked her, "What's the matter?" She said, "I went to the bathroom and when I came out the theater was closed and all the doors are locked, and I can't get out." I said, "Well, go to the back of the theater and there should be a emergency exit door there with a push bar on it. Just push the handle and it should open." We'll walk back there to make sure you get out. If not, come back here and we'll find a phone and get some help."

So we walked around the side to the back, and sure enough there was a door there and soon she came out. Boy, was she appreciative. She gave Ajan a hug; then she gave me a hug and she whispered in my ear, "Want me to come with you?" I said, "no thanks. I had always figured, "I had steak at home, I didn't need hamburger on the road." I was totally in love with my wife and kids and just wouldn't have been able to look them in the eyes if I had "cheated" on them.

As much as I traveled, when I was married I never bought a drink for or danced with another woman. I got to thinking later, "I wonder how many times she's pulled the "locked in the theater trick?"

Johnson left his BSA out at my trailer for fear of it getting stolen at the base. If you had to leave your car parked just outside the main gate overnight, (for getting kicked off the base for speeding or something) you'd probably find it sitting on the road, with the wheels gone by morning! I used to see that quite often! Johnson said I could ride the BSA whenever I wanted to. (I suppose he figured if I hadn't totaled it while I was half drunk on Okinawa, it was safe to leave it with me now that I wasn't drinking much!)

He would come out and ride the BSA every once in while and we'd have him stay for supper. And sometimes we'd pull out the "hide-a-bed" and he'd spend the night with us. After he met Peggy, we didn't see much of him anymore! I wondered, ("Hmmm, is Johnson out of love with that twenty ton crane, and in love with Peggy??")

But I made sure the BSA didn't get rusty for him! I'd met a few other guys in the area who had motorcycles. We'd

Johnson on his BSA next to my 52 Oldsmobile at my trailer house.

meet out at Fort Washington, which was about five miles from my trailer. Out at the "Fort", as we called it, they had some old, ammunition bunkers that they used to store ammunition in--way back in the civil war days I guess. About four to six of us would play chase and of course it was great fun to go up and over these ammo bunkers, up and down hills, or steps, gun mounts, whatever! Not to mention in and around trees and bushes!

It was just a matter of time, I guess, until whoever was doing the grounds keeping reported our tracks and abuse to the lawns to someone.

A couple of months later we had some friends out for Sunday dinner. Afterward Dave and I went outside while the "girls" did the dishes. (I always figured, "They made the mess; they can clean it up!") I showed Dave, Johnson's BSA alongside the house and asked if he'd like to go for a ride. So we got on and I headed out to the "Fort." When we got there, it was pretty much, full of cars and people picnicking all over the place! "How the hell was I going to give Dave

a ride up and over an "ammo bunker" like this I thought! There was a "road closed" barrier about halfway across the

Who could ever blame us for wanting to ride motor cycles on top of this??!!

road at the entrance so I just wheeled around it, of course!
About fifty feet later I saw a motorcycle cop coming across
the grass right toward me! It didn't take any rocket scientist
to figure out that he was anxious to talk to me!

My first thought was, "If I didn't have Dave on the back
I'd turn around and leave that Harley in the dust! But for
once I showed good judgment and shut it down and waited
for the cop to get there. The cop said, "Didn't you see that
"road closed" barrier over there?" I said, "Yeah, I saw it. I
also noticed it was only halfway across the road and all
those cars were parked beyond it so I thought the road must
be open."

He started in on me then, "Don't get smart with me.
Where's your registration?!" He got a little more madder
when I didn't have any registration! He said, "It's probably a
stolen motorcycle and, I bet, "You're one of them damn
hoodlums that's out here at night tearing up the grass!" Boy,
he was mad. "He must have been a TI the way he was chewing my ass," I thought!

"Where do you live, where do you work? What rank are
you?" I told him I was an Airmen First. "Well, you'll be an

Airmen Basic when I get done with you!" he said. I almost told him "Lots of luck." I knew damn well Colonel Steffes, wouldn't let that happen. He gave me a ticket for something and we left.

I rode back home and Dave and his wife went home. So I got the registration and rode back out to the "Fort" and found this cop again. I rode up and shut down along side facing him. I said, "Here's the registration you didn't think I had." And I said, "I don't think I deserved the ass chewing you gave me in front of my friend, for going around a barrier, that obviously all those other cars had gone around. And I don't like to be embarrassed in front of one of my friends by you threatening that you're going to have me busted and calling me a hoodlum! So, I said, "I'll show you where I work and who I work for," and I handed him the letter of appreciation, I had recently received from Colonel Steffes.

I said, "I bet if Colonel Steffes makes a phone call from the Pentagon to your precinct police captain you'll be walking a beat down in the slums." So I said, "Let's see who gets who busted first!"

I was pissed! I started up the BSA, ready to ride off and he said, "How about if I just tear the ticket up and we forget it? I said, "The war's off then." He said, "OK." I rode away thinking, "You've got more guts than sense Hubbell." Luckily he never asked me, if, in fact, I was one of those "hoodlums", or I would have had to give him an honest, straight answer.

I remember coming back from the Springs, as we called it now, and our number "2" airplane was across the other side of the base for some periodical inspections including prop overhauls, etc. Delroy, said to me, "Les, we've got a problem with number "2" and it's got a flight tomorrow afternoon!"(It wouldn't look good to the Pentagon if one of our airplanes didn't make a scheduled flight!) I asked, "What's the matter?" He said, "Every time we run it up and

REPLY TO
ATTN OF: OG 1/Col Etter/238   27 Jul 1959

SUBJECT: Letter of Appreciation

TO: 1100 Maint & Sup Gp (M&S 20).

1. The attached correspondence received from Lt. Colonel E. Q. Steffes, Aide-de-Camp to the Vice Chief of Staff, is forwarded for your information.

2. Crew chiefs for the Vice Chief of Staff's Flight were:

T/Sgt Delroy R. Mills;	S/Sgt Ronald R. Young
S/Sgt Bruce A. Currie	S/Sgt Rhuel Sperry
S/Sgt Joseph M. Dungan	S/Sgt Louis E. Ajjan
A/1C Leslie V. Hubbell	

3. Please extend my personal appreciation to these airmen for their fine co-operation and assistance.

RICHARD W. ETTER
Colonel, USAF
Commander

1 Atch
Ltr, DAF, 14 Jul 59

letter of appreciation from Colonel Steffes

go to high rpm, the props go into feather." The props have been off twice and back to the prop shop, but we've still got the problem. What do you think that is?" "Boy, damned if I know, Delroy," I said. Besides it was late and I was tired, and horny, and wanted to go home. I woke up in the middle of the night, no longer horny, thinking about the problem with number "2" and what they might have done. I was out to the office by six in the morning; Delroy was already there. I asked Delroy, "Do I remember hearing you say that they were going to change out the prop control switches on number "2"?" He said, "Yes, they did." I got a maintenance manual and looked up the wiring diagram for the switches and told Delroy that I thought the problem was that they've got wires "A" and "B" reversed on the prop control switches. Delroy said, in that slow Oklahoma drawl, "Well, I'll be a son of a bitch" and called over to the electrical shop. An hour later they had the problem fixed and the aircraft run up and ready to go! "One of my better moments!" I remember thinking, "Maybe I'm only the 200th dumbest kid in the world!

I remember DelRoy calling over to the electrical shop a few minutes later and talking to the sergeant in charge of it. DelRoy just enjoyed the hell out of chewing somebody's ass for anything, in that Oklahoma drawl he had. He and this other sergeant must have been good friends because DelRoy was saying, "what the f--- kinda electrical shop are you stupid "muverfuger's" running over there anyway?! You can't even wire a simple damn switch! And, to make matters worse, you can't even recognize your own f--- --g mistakes!! And I've got a kid over here off a farm in Minnesota, that's not even a electrician, that figures the problem out in his sleep! He didn't even have to come over there and look at nothing!! I'll tell you what I'm going to do for you "dumb sob's", the next time you f--- something up, and can't find the problem, you just call me and I'll run it by this kid. Now I'll tell you right up front, it ain't going to be cheap, and if you need the answer right way bring cash because I ain't taking your check, because your check probably ain't no better than you are. (I always wondered if DelRoy got as much enjoyment out of chewing someone's ass, as he did having sex!)

Johnson was a crew chief on a gooney bird in the next squadron, just a couple of blocks to the south of where I was working. One of their gooney birds had lost an engine up over West Virginia and had landed at Martinsburg, West Virginia. Johnson and a couple of other guys had taken an engine up there and changed it out. During the time they were there for those few days, they'd eat at a local café of course. As it turned out, there was a pretty little waitress with dark hair working there, named Peggy. Johnson asked me one day if I'd take a flight for him on the DC 3 that he was crewing because he wanted to go up to Martinsburg to see Peggy. I told him, "I don't know anything about DC3's." He said, "You don't know much about Convairs either but they let you fly on them." Then he went on to explain that the crew chief on a "3" doesn't start the engines and handle the power etc., like we did on the Convairs. He said, "You just have to be there in case some mechanical problem arises during the flight. Mostly you just stand around and look like you know what you're doing." Then he added, "and you've got that perfected," so I took the flight for him.

It turned out the flight was a couple of lieutenants getting their four hours of flying time in for the month. We took off from Bolling and flew four hours west and landed someplace for fuel. They changed seats and we flew four hours east back to Bolling. They did that all at about seven to nine thousand feet. It was rougher than hell, hotter than hell, noisier than hell, no bathroom, just a "relief tube" and didn't even have a flight steward, just box lunches! When Johnson got back I said, "Don't ever ask me to fly on one of them SOB's again!" (I was spoiled by all the comforts the Convair had, including air conditioning!)

Well one thing led to another and I was best man when Johnson married Peggy Allen on March 29, 1959 in Martinsburg, West Virginia! (I would guess that the best thing Johnson ever did was to join the Air Force too, because they sure have had a great marriage.) That was the first time I met Johnson's parents, Evert and Edith Johnson. They had driven out from Erwin, South Dakota in their brand new 1959 Chevrolet Impala, for the wedding. They spent the night on our hide-a-bed and we drove up to Martinsburg the next day.

I had a 1952 Super 88 Oldsmobile and had all I could do to keep up with Evert! The road was up and down and around corners and my wheels were squealing on half the turns! When we got there, glad to be alive, Evert got out and said to me, "You did pretty good; you kept up!" I was to learn later that "that's how they drive all the time in South Dakota!"

A few months before my four years of duty was to end, Colonel Steffes came over one day and asked me if would like to go to Officer Candidate School and flight training? I knew the wife's folks wanted us to come home and for me to work in their grocery store. Besides, she was an only child and I guess I thought it would be nice for them to have their daughter and grandchildren near so I turned that opportunity down.

I've pondered that decision several times. If I had gone to OCS and flight training I'd have been "ripe" for Vietnam. Either one of two things might have happened. I wasn't in favor of that war, as least the way we were fighting it, so I might have loaded up an F100 with all the armament she could carry and flown to Hanoi and blown Ho Chi Minh off the map and probably gone to Levenworth. Or, I might have gotten a SAM up my tailpipe and never come home.

So I said goodbye to everyone and headed back to Minnesota about the tenth of October 1959. Delroy had told me he'd keep my job open for ninety days if I decided to come back. I thanked him for that.

Johnson and Peggy loaded up and moved back to farm in Erwin about the same time we left for Minnesota.

Chapter Eight

Back Home
1959

When I got home, my Dad had two Champs. He had a "65" horse and then he had found a "75" horse that he liked better, and hadn't sold the "65" yet.

My initial flight training consisted of a few lessons from my older brother, who had gotten out of the Air Force a year before me and had his private license. After that we had a great time chasing each other down the pipeline, around trees, buzzing our friends, whatever! But one day, my Dad saw us dog fighting over the Cloquet airport! I heard him tell people several times, "I came out to the airport and there was them two boys dog fighting over the airport!" He said that he went home and told Ma, "I've got to sell one of them airplanes before them boys kill themselves!" There went our fun!

Johnson had invited me to come out pheasant hunting the end of October so my Dad and I flew out there in his 75

My Dad warming up his Champ

horse. We "buzzed" Evert's farm and then went on down to Lake Preston and landed. It wasn't long before Johnson and Evert were there to pick us up.

Johnson and Peggy were living with Edith and Evert until they could get moved into his grandparents' old farm about a mile north, so we had the "basement suite." We had a great supper and a nice visit before turning in. The next morning we drove down to Johnson's brother's farm south of Iroquois, around where the old town of Esmond used to be, to hunt.

His brother Linell, who was ten years older than Johnson, was a super nice guy. There were about fifteen other guys there – some from as far away as North Carolina! Linell was "the trail boss;" he'd have the whole hunt arranged. He'd tell us what field we were going to hunt and which way we were going to walk it and he'd call for how many blockers we'd need. My dad and the rest of the older guys would be the blockers. The rest of us were walkers. He'd drop the walkers off first. Then he and the blockers would drive to the far end. I had never hunted pheasants before and I couldn't believe how many there were! There would be so many getting up it was hard to decide which one to shoot at! Then there would be the roosters that would get up right along side me, cackling like crazy and startling the hell out of me! By the time I figured out what was happening, they were gone! My dad and I managed to get our limits! Of course you could "flock shoot," there were so many of them, and do that!

Before lunch was the first time I heard Evert tell the story about "the old farmer that went to church in the middle of a blizzard." He said, "Even though there was a raging blizzard going on, this old farmer went to church, out in the country. He and the minister were the only ones there. The only reason the minister was there was because he lived right next to the church. The minister kept going from the pulpit to a window and would look out to see if anyone else was coming. He did that until about twenty minutes after nine and then he went down to the old farmer and said, "I don't know if I should give the sermon or not with only one person in church. What do you think?" The old farmer slowly said, "Well, if I went out to feed my cows and only one cow showed up, I'd feed her." The minister said, "You're right." So he preached and preached and preached for an hour and a half! When he was done, he went down to the old farmer and asked him how he had liked the sermon. The old farmer again slowly said, "Well, if I went out to feed my cows and only one cow showed up, I'd feed her, but I wouldn't give her the whole dang load!" Only Evert could tell that story, the way he did, and I laughed as much the last time I heard him tell it as I did the first time!

We hunted down at Linell's for two days. After we were done hunting each day, Linell's wife Lilly and the other ladies had a great meal prepared for us. Sunday afternoon Dad and I headed back to Cloquet, in his Champ. We were bucking a good headwind and it was snowing and getting dark by the time we got to Isle, on the southeast corner of Millacs Lake so we decided to land there and spend the night. There were so many deer on the runway we had to make a low pass to shag them off the runway before we could land. It was just a short walk to a place we could rent a cabin for the night. The next morning we had breakfast and were home by 10:30.

I hunted with Johnson and Evert many times after that first time down at Linell's place. Then we'd hunt Evert's tree line when we got back to Erwin. I was always amazed at how many pheasants we'd kick out of that tree line too! We'd pretty much always get out limit. There were some years when hunting was a little slow, but the Johnsons – Evert, Linell and Mel as I'd call him when there were twenty other Johnson's around, would make sure I went home with my limit.

The next summer, 1960, I began taking flying lessons up at Duluth Airways while I was working at the store. I'd get up there early and then work late, or vise versa. My instructor was Bud Randall and the trainer was a Cessna 120. Things went pretty good until one day we were doing "stop and goes" on runway "09" at Duluth. Bud had helped me with a couple and this was going to be the first one by myself he said, as he sat back and crossed his arms across his chest. (I'm thinking, maybe he's the dumbest kid in the world!) So I came in and planted that little 120 firmly on runway "09", the nose was going left and right and the tires were squealing. I went off the left side of the runway. Once I got on the grass, I got it straightened out, cut back onto the runway between the next set of lights and parked it on the centerline!

Bud was still sitting there with his arms crossed and I said, "Keep your damn feet off the brakes!" He said, "I don't have any brakes on my side." I said, "You better get some damn brakes then!" Not long after that I had that little 120 tamed and Bud got out and said, "Take her around for three takeoffs and landings." (Now I was sure he's "the dumbest kid in the world!")

I even remembered to call the tower!. Bud had told me that they'd had a couple people who were so excited to solo, they forgot to call the tower! The takeoff went good, but once up in the pattern and on downwind I found myself wondering, "How the hell am I going to get this thing back on the runway without wrecking it?! Somehow, I did my three takeoffs and landings and kept it on its wheels! And on October 16, 1960 I found out to my surprise that "I wasn't too dumb to be a pilot!"

My dad was a great pilot, he flew like a bird, always

knew where he was. He could land that Champ on a dime. He'd take my mother and fly down to Urbana, Ill to visit my oldest sister, he'd take his paper mill buddies ice fishing up on the Whitefish chain, gave anyone that wanted one, a ride, etc. He only had one "little" flaw, he never had a license! (Hmmm, I wonder if that's why, "I color outside the lines a little" as my friend Linda, likes to remind me of once in awhile?)

A few years later when I had an instructor rating, I offered to help him get through the written several times, but he just wanted to fly. He owned three different airplanes and flew for thirteen years before he decided to quit while he was ahead! He was as good or better "stick and rudder" pilot as anyone I've ever flown with! In fact I don't remember him ever making a less than "perfect landing!" (I wish I could say that about myself!)

Chapter Nine

Working in the-in-laws Grocery Store
Nov 1959 - June 1960

Well, ninety days went by so fast. I had only been working in the store for about sixty days.. I could tell my father-in-law was proud to introduce me to his customers and to have me there. At first it was "kinda fun" and I was "OK" being there. The help and the customers were nice. I remember Ronnie Algren, who was going to college then. I was behind the meat counter and Ronnie was stocking shelves out front of me about fifteen feet when a lady, who was a longtime customer, came down the aisle and asked Ronnie where the charcoal lighter was at. Ronnie said, "It's right around the corner next to the wall." She found the charcoal lighter and asked, "How much are they?" Ronnie said, "Forty nine cents." She said, "Well, ain't they two for something like downtown?" Ronnie replied, "Yes, they're two for ninety eight cents." And she said, "Good, I'll take two!" I suspect Ronnie did good in college!

My father in-law had a 1957 Mercury station wagon. That sucker wouldn't start if a cloud went over. One cold winter Sunday morning, he and the mother-in-law were going to go to church and later to Duluth to visit relatives, but the Mercury wouldn't start. The father-in-law came back to the butcher shop and asked if he could use my Oldsmobile to go to church. I said, "Of course" and walked home a block away and brought it over to the store. Their living quarters were attached to the store. He asked me if I'd get his Mercury warmed up while they were gone to church so he could drive it to Duluth. I said, "No problem!"

They left and I went down to the basement and found a blowtorch and an empty metal gallon can. I cut the can open and flattened it our so I had a piece of metal about six inches wide and a foot long. I wired it to the blowtorch and "lit her up!" I had bent the end of the metal up a little so the heat would hit it and "bounce up". I was proud of my invention! I took it outside and opened the hood of the Mercury and put the, "MBEH" (Modified Blowtorch Engine Heater) as we would have called it in the Air Force, underneath the front of the oil pan. I watched it for a few minutes and I could see the frost starting to come out of the block. It was working great!! One of my better ideas! I thought, "Maybe I should have been a rocket scientist," and lowered the hood and went back to the butcher shop. About ten minutes later a customer came into the store saying there was "smoke coming form under the hood of Carl's Mercury!" I grabbed the only fire extinguisher in the store, a little one about three inches wide and maybe six inches high. I ran out there and opened the hood and the hoses, fan belts, wiring and anything that could burn was burning! I turned that little fire extinguisher on and it, "pee'd" out a little stream! I could have done better myself! I grabbed a snow shovel and after about six shovels full of snow I had the fire out. I closed the hood and went back into the store.

About forty five minutes later, the father-in-law came back to the meat counter and asked me if I had gotten the Mercury warmed up. I said, "Yeah, I did." He said "Good, I'll drive it to Duluth then." "Naw, go ahead and drive my car as long as it's warmed up," I said. "No," he said, "I'll take the Mercury. It'll be good for it to charge the battery up." "Yeah," it would," I said, "but it needs a fan belt." You'd had to have known Carl, he was the easiest going guy there ever was. Then he gets me for a son-in-law! He said, "Well maybe Cool's Implement across the street might have one." I said, "They might, but it needs a power steering hose too." He said, "I wonder if they'd have that? If not, they could probably make one," he said. I said, "Yeah, but I think it needs a fuel pump and hoses too." He said, "I'll go over and see what they've got" I said, "Yeah, but it's too damn cold to rewire it today." He looked at me with a kind off a blank stare, and said, "Are you trying to tell me something?" So I told him what had happened and he said, "You're right, I'll take your car."

He had the Mercury fixed and never said a word to me about what it cost. But, I was letting his daughter sleep with me so that had to be worth something to him, I figured! I mean, it's got to be really hard to find a son-in-law with a sense of humor who will let your daughter sleep with him!

The next summer we had his boat hooked to the Mercury and went fishing up on Leech Lake. Coming back, he ran out of gas on Highway 33 about 7 miles north of Cloquet. (It sure wasn't my fault he hadn't gotten the fuel gauge fixed after the fire!) But, no problem, we had gas for the outboard motor in the boat. He went and got the can while I took the air cleaner off. He poured about four gallons in the gas tank and then I poured about a cupful down the carburetor and said, "Hit her Carl." He did, and she was on fire again! We picked up sand with our hands and put on it, and got it out. He looked at me and said, "You really hate this car, don't you?" I bet he was thinking, "I wish my daughter had married some other guy." (Unbeknownst to me, twenty years later I would be wishing that same thing!)

It was maybe about May of 1960 and he was showing me how to cut up a hind quarter of beef. If you do it just right, you end up with a piece of the hind joint about the size of a quarter. He'd done that and was pleased.

I was standing there thinking, "What the hell am I doing here?" I knew, then and there, that it wasn't going to work out because I just couldn't stand being cooped up inside all day. It was going to hurt me to tell Carl that because he had hopes of us taking over the store someday and he'd been so good to me.

He had an accountant from Minneapolis who had bought a motel and trailer park up the road a couple of blocks and he had people managing it for him. I confided in him one day that I was going to have to tell Carl that I wasn't cut out for working in the store. He said he was losing money on the motel and trailer park because he couldn't get the people to work. All they'd do is call a plumber or electrician or painter or whatever, and send him the bills. He said, "I'll sell you Sunnyside." I said, "OK, a dollar down and a dollar a month and I'll take it." Carl loaned us $9,000 and we bought a motel and trailer park!

Chapter Ten

Sunnyside Motel and Trailer Park
July 1960-May 1969

So there we were, "two kids, with two kids," in two different businesses at the same time – the Motel and Trailer Park business! I was 23 and she was 22. Neither of us knew a thing about running a business! About all we knew to start with was if we had empty rooms, turn the vacancy sign on, if we were filled up, turn the "no vacancy" sign on. I guess it didn't take a rocket scientist to figure that out though! Then the next morning, clean the dirty rooms, and rent them again the next night! Not too hard so far!

Sunnyside Motel

The wife pretty much ran the motel and her aunt did the cleaning. I was busy with the trailer park. It had about thirty six trailers in it. There was a small dumpster near the entrance to the park for people to climb up four or five steps and dump their garbage in. Of course some would spill on the ground and that attracted rats. I had seen several of them out there at night.

So about the first thing I did was have people buy their own thirty gallon trash containers and have one out front of their trailer where the garbage man could pick it up and empty it. Boy was I considered a "SOB" for that! I heard several times that "You should provide the cans" and "That ain't the way the former owner did it!" I got to where I'd tell people, "I'm sorry, but he ain't here anymore and neither are the rats!" But I guess we all resist change.

One day, a few months after we had bought the business, I came home and the wife was crying. I asked her, "What's the matter, honey?"(I'm a "softy" when women cry.) She said a guy had checked into the motel and gave her a hard time about the price and wanted to talk to the boss. She said she was the boss and he wouldn't believe her because she was so young. He said, "The lady on the phone must be the boss." My wife said, "No, she's my aunt. She does the cleaning and I'm the owner." Her aunt verified that. My wife was about eight months pregnant and I didn't appreciate whoever this was giving her a hard time and causing her to cry.

Our commercial rate was $6.00 at that time, so I took $6.00 out of the till and went and knocked on the man's door. I got a grumpy, "Who is it?" And I said, "The owner." He opened the door and even more grumpily asked "What do you want?" I said, "My wife is over there crying because you gave her a hard time about the price of the room and I want you to take your six dollars here and go downtown to the hotel where you can get a room for two dollars. He said,

"Oh, I'm sorry Mr. Hubbell, your rooms are really nice. I like it here." I said, "Don't apologize to me, I ain't the one that's crying. If you really mean it, pick up the phone on the desk over there and tell her that." He did that and he came back many times after. I had already learned that "the customer is not always right!" I would go a long way with people if they were tired and a little grumpy. But I didn't cut any slack for a drunk or a cheapskate.

One night, in the summer, about 11 P.M. I was taking care of the motel and an older couple from Missouri checked in. I was taking them out to the motel to show them to their room. They must not have had birch trees where they lived. And it was too dark for them to have seen them along the highway while they were driving, because the wife looked at my front yard full of nice white birch trees and asked, "What do you do, paint your trees? I said, "Yes ma'am, it gets kind of slow around here sometimes and it gives me something to do."

Another time three "little old ladies" checked in while I was on duty at the front desk. It was a late Thursday afternoon and I was taking them out to show them their rooms. The wind was out of the southeast, so we were getting the "paper mill smell." One of the little old ladies said, "My gosh sonny, what is that smell?" I don't know where I come up with all this "garbage," but I said, "Well, Cloquet is just about one hundred percent German, and every Thursday afternoon everybody makes sauerkraut. One of them said, "That's what I like about small towns. People still do stuff like that. Ain't that nice!! (The paper mill had always smelled like sauerkraut to me!)

The motel had that old blond metal furniture in it. I mean, it already looked old in 1961! So that winter, I went down to the Eckberg Lumber Company and made a deal with them that if I could use their shop, I'd buy all of my materials from them. That was OK with them and I spent most of the

The remodeled motel rooms at the Sunnyside Motel.

winter between snow plowing, fixing frozen water lines, fixing this, fixing that, etc., making six wall mounted desks, twelve wall mounted seats with blanket storage space, six wall mounted headboards and six matching diamond shaped reading light holders.

One of the wife's uncles, Wayne Vargason, had a service station and also made wrought iron railings. So I went down there and he let me use his equipment and I made six wall mounted corner TV stands. I mounted them high enough so you could see the TV without having to look between your toes! I installed a pull switch between the reading light pull switches to turn the TV on and off from in bed even! That was before remotes, so it was nice to be able to at least turn the TV on or off without getting out of bed. We were "high tech" I figured. That furniture is still in the first six units of Sunnyside Motel in Cloquet yet today. I stayed there in 1995 for my fortieth high school class reunion and it was weird to lay there and look at stuff I had made thirty four years ago! I asked Mary, the owner back then, if they had any plans to replace it and she said, "Why? We still get compliments on it!"

The trailer park came with three rental units. One of them we rented to Peggy and Leona. They both worked in the office down at the paper mill. If I remember right they rented from us for about two years and then they both got married. We lost track of Peggy, but Leona married Dave Johnson who also worked at the paper mill. ("Hmmm," I always wondered, "was he dipping his pen in company ink?") We used to get together often and enjoyed playing hearts and having a few drinks every now and then and had become good friends. After they got married, they bought a house a couple miles east of Esko, Minnesota. And of course, they started having kids, just like we were, ("I quit hmmm'ing.") Our paths grew apart. These last few years I've stopped to visit them and I make a low pass over their house once in awhile with my 310 to let them know I'm in the area and thinking about them. (Low pass: 1,000 feet above the highest obstacle within a 2000 foot radius.)

I rented our smallest trailer house to a newlywed young couple with a baby who was about a month old. I could never figure out why this girl had married this kid. He just looked like a loser to me. (Of course, maybe I didn't look too sharp to him either!) Come to think about it, he worked at the paper mill. (Hmmm, I wonder if she had too?) He paid the first month's rent when they moved in but after that every month it was a dogfight to collect the rent. If it hadn't been for feeling sorry for the girl and her little baby, I would have evicted this kid in a minute, but I felt sorry for her. After about three months of this though I was wearing thin and his rent was three or four days late again. I went down and knocked on his door and reminded him that his rent was past due again. I explained to him that I was responsible for and had to pay all the electrical bills for the whole thirty six homes in the park. (Thank God, that changed later.) And I said, "If people didn't pay me, I can't pay the power company". I asked him when he could pay his rent and he said, "Next Friday is paper mill payday." He said he'd pay me then." Well, next Friday came and went and I waited a day or two before I went down and knocked on the door again and reminded this kid, who was maybe four years younger than I was then, (he's probably still four years younger than me, come to think about it) that he hadn't paid his rent as promised, again. He gave me a story about having all these bills to pay etc., and I invited him up to the office to see all the bills I had to pay and again reminded him that "I can't pay mine if you don't pay me!" So I asked him, once again, "When is paper mill payday and what shift will you be working?" Paper mill payday was going to be on the fifteenth and he'd be working the day shift. So I said, "OK, can we agree then that you will have your rent paid in full by 6 P.M. on the fifteenth. He agreed. And I said, "do you understand that if it is not paid by 6 P.M on the fifteenth, I am going to put a padlock on your electrical box?" He said that he understood.

Well, 6 P.M. on the fifteenth came and went, so did 7 P.M. and then 8 P.M. I got a padlock and walked down there. Nobody was home. That made it easier for me because I couldn't have done it if that girl was home alone with her little baby. Besides this was in January or February and it was about zero outside! I "pulled the power" as we called it back then, and put a padlock on the box. I knew it wouldn't be long and the water line would freeze too. (I don't know if there were laws against doing this back then or not, but I probably would have done it anyway.)

Well, about 10:30 P.M. the phone rang and this kid says, "I don't have any water or electricity down here!" I said, "Do you know what day and time it is? He asked, "Is that my box out there with the padlock on it?" I said, "Yes it is." He said, "I'm going to go out there and pull it off the post!" I said, "You do, and I'm going to come down there and break your f...ing neck!." (Try getting away with that today!) He said, "What do I have to do to get my water and power back? (Now I knew this kid wasn't rocket scientist material for sure.) So I said, "Paying your rent might work?" He hung up and about thirty minutes later he was at the door with the rent, cash, paid in full! I gave him a receipt and told him, "We're not going to play this game anymore and if you're ever late again, you're gone." That kid paid his rent on time for the rest of the time they lived there! I thought after, "Maybe I should go to charm school and learn more about being nice to people." But then I thought, "I had been nice; that didn't work; being down and dirty worked!"

I was pretty busy with the trailer park, digging up broken water lines, replacing collapsed sewer lines, moving homes in and out of the park; and the wife was busy with the motel.

By this time Drs. Byron and Lloyd Backus and I had our private pilot licenses, so we bought a Cessna 170A, N9006A, together. I remember being up at the hospital in the room with the wife, awaiting the birth of our fourth child and Dr. Lloyd and I were looking out the window at a airplane flying by and she said, "Remember me you guys; I'm here to have a baby!" I knew right then and there that she had her priorities all wrong!!

In October of 1961 I had the family loaded in the car, all ready to drive out to Erwin, South Dakota to visit Johnson and Peggy and do a little pheasant hunting. A package had come for someone in the park so I put it in the car, drove down to the trailer park, and gave it to the lady. As I was walking away she said, "Oh, Les, there's water coming up in my yard." I walked over and looked, sure enough, there was water coming up in her yard.

So I drove back up to the house, and the wife and kids went inside, and I changed clothes and got a shovel and a rake. This was going to be about the fourth one of these that I had fixed already so I had it down to a science. (Hmmm, maybe God was preparing me to be a rocket scientist?")

The trailer park had originally been built just to park the trailer houses and travel trailers for workers of the Williams Pipe Line Company for the couple of years that they were going to be in the area. So it had been built cheap. The sewer lines were "orangeburg pipe" which consisted of nothing more than about six layers of tar paper and tar rolled up in four to eight foot lengths. The water lines were 3/4 inch galvanized pipe. Worse yet, they were both buried in the same trench, only three to four feet deep and back-filled with sawdust and two to three feet of dirt. That made then easy to dig up, but after digging the first one I wondered how the health department had let this park stay open. Even at 24 years old I knew this was a health hazard and I was going to have to either close it or build a new park!

It only took about fifteen minutes to dig down to the water line and expose the cracked or broken pipe. Then I'd take bleach and "disinfect" the pipe with it, for about two feet on each side of where I was going cut it. Then I'd cut it, slide on a 3/4 inch splice like the gas company used, tighten it up, test it, back-fill it. I did all that and we were out of there in a little over an hour and back on the road to South Dakota!

We got there before supper time and Peggy had a nice meal made for us. The next morning Johnson, his dad Evert and I were driving down to Johnson's brother, Linell's farm, at Carthage, South Dakota, about thirty miles southwest of Erwin and about the same distance southeast of Huron, South Dakota. Evert was driving, Johnson was in the front seat and I was in the backseat. We were going down a dirt road and I thought, "Boy, we're clipping." I looked around Evert at the speedometer; we were doing seventy miles an hour! I said, "Do you guys always drive seventy miles an hour down these dirt roads?" Johnson looked back at me, with a puzzled look and said, "This ain't no dirt road; this is a county road." I thought, "Oh excuse me, I thought it must be the "South Dakota 500!" I thought, "If they drive this fast on a county road, I bet they do a hundred twenty five on a state road!" I was wrong, they only did eight to eighty-five maybe!

Every year for quite awhile, when I'd go out there pheasant hunting, it became my job to climb up Evert's wind generator tower, and grease whatever needed greasing. It was the same as a windmill but instead of a pump jack it turned a generator. I remember Johnson showing me a bunch of batteries in the basement of Evert's house. The only thing I couldn't figure out though was, "How can these guys drive seventy miles an hour down those dirt roads and then be scared to climb a fifty foot wind generator tower!"

We always had a nice visit with Johnson and Peggy and the whole Johnson family. I've often thought, "If I hadn't joined the Air Force I'd never have met Johnson, Peggy, Evert, Edith, Linell, Lilly and their families, who had all become such important people in my life! Yes, joining the Air Force was one of the best things I had ever done!

Every time I'd have to dig up another broken water line I realized, more and more, that I had to build a new trailer park and shut this health hazard down! I've thought back on it and, I never gave a thought to suing the former owner to get my money back. I just started looking around for about ten acres to buy to build a new trailer park on. I didn't even think about where I was going to get the money to build it, I just figured, " Where there's a will, there's a way!" (I know God has looked down at me several times and thought, "This kid ain't very bright; I better give him some help.") I've also thought, over the years, "I sure hope that when I meet God, he has a sense of humor or he's going to be really ticked at some of the jokes I've told!"

About mid-summer, 1962, Mr. Peterson, who lived just a couple hundred feet southwest of my house, came over one day. He said, "Les, I own the twelve acres that butts up against your property to the west there," as he pointed to the nice birch covered hill and woods that I could see out my back door. He said, "My wife and I always planned on building a house up on that birch hill, but we've decided were not going to do that now and were going to sell it." He went on to say, "Les, you're a young business man and I'd like you to have first chance to buy that piece of land." I asked, "How much do you want for it?" and he said, "$1,500.00." ($1,500.00 dollars back in 1962 was still considered a fair amount of money and I didn't have it!) I told him, "I'm broke right now with having just bought the business and making improvements, but I'd see what I could do."

He said he'd give me a first refusal for ten days to see if I could get the money before he listed it with a realtor, and I thanked him. (Yes, I can be polite now and then, especially when I think I'm going to profit from something!) After he left, I called my banker, Ted Micke, who was also one of my best friends. We had been in JC's, played ping pong and socialized as couples together. Ted knew I was looking for a piece of land, so when I called him and told him about Mr. Peterson coming over and offering to sell me the twelve acres next to my land for $1,500 dollars, he said, "Write him a check!" Now, he knew I didn't have "two nickels to rub together" and he still said, "Write him a check!" I'm thinking to myself, ("Hmmm, I wonder if Ted's the dumbest kid in the world.") So I waited a few days, so as not to appear to be too anxious, and then went over and told Mr. Peterson that apparently my banker is dumber than me and made me a loan to buy his land. So now I had a piece of land, dropped right into my lap, right out the back door, of my house, that I could build a new trailer park on! Is that luck or what? Or (Hmmm, was God looking down at me again, I wondered.)

So, I drew up the plans for a thirty three lot trailer park to fit on the south half of the land I had just bought. Now, I'm not an engineer, or a plumber, or an electrician or an equipment operator or nothing, I'm just a "dumb kid," from off the farm, but I figured if I know what I wanted to end up with, I could figure out how to build it!

The city sewer out in the front ditch was only four feet below the ditch so I knew I was going to need a sewage lift station to pump the sewage from the park up to the city sewer. Harry Petersen, the plumber who I was buying my plumbing supplies from found a used lift station for me. When I got my plans done and figured out that it was going to cost $15,000, I went down to the bank to apply for a loan. I gave Ted the information I had and he in took it to the loan committee.

I stopped by the bank a week later. Ted was out, so I talked to Mr. McCastle, who was the owner and president of the bank. I asked him, "Mac, have you made a decision on my loan yet?" He said, "Les you haven't had that business more than two years now and we'd like to see how your financials look in another year or two before we approve a loan to build a new park." My wife wasn't supportive of me building a new park, and now the banker wasn't either! I said, "Mac, I'm going to build this park with or without you, so think about it and I'll be back next week." (I knew I wasn't the smartest kid around, but at least I had guts!)

I had worked for the Stewart Furniture Company, delivering furniture during my junior year in school and the Stewarts had just opened a new bank in town, the City National Bank. I had run into Jerry Stewart at the café, having lunch one day, and had told him I was going to build a new trailer park, and he wanted to know if he could finance it. I told him Ted and I were good friends, and I needed to give First National first chance. He said, "If you have any problem come see me."

So when Mac said they thought I should wait a year or two, I went back down and talked to Jerry and showed him my plans, financials etc. He said he'd do it. In fact he wanted all my business so we made a verbal agreement.

A couple of days later I went back into First National. I had already talked to Ted on the phone, and went into Mac's office and asked him if they had changed their mind. He said, "No, the decision was firm." So I said, "Figure up what I owe you and I'll bring you a check." He asked, "How are you going to do that?" and I told him. He said, "Well maybe we should take another look at this." I said, "You're too late Mac, give me a number and I'll go get a check," which I did. So now I've got the plans and the money but I don't even have my plans approved by the state yet! ("Hmmm, maybe I am the dumbest kid in the world, I thought.")

Any plans over $10,000 needed to be approved by a registered engineer, which wasn't me, so I took them down to Bruce Boyer who was the city engineer. He looked them over, didn't make any changes, put his stamp on them and sent them down to the state. The state had them for about a month and sent them back to me "approved!"

So now I had the money and my plans approved so I went and bought a "transit" and taught myself how to use it. I had a couple of tenants who were also good friends, Herbie Bromme, and Dave Maunu. I hired them to help me when they had time.

There was also a guy by the name of Joe Adams living in the park. He was living alone. He was about sixty-five years old and had a pin in his left knee and was always in pain. He had nothing else to do and would help me do whatever I was doing just to get out and move around. He was my right hand man. It was nice to have him around to hand me tools when I was under a mobile home or in a ditch building the trailer park, etc. I didn't charge him lot rent in exchange for his help. He'd be up all night playing solitaire and taking pain pills. I had him programmed to call me at 5 A.M. if we got 4 four inches or more of snow. By the time I got up and wolfed down a bowl of cereal and got outside, he'd have the truck warmed up, swept off and a cup of coffee waiting for me! It was nice to have Joe around to help me. (Hmmm, had God looked down and provided the help I needed??)

One day I was taking care of the motel office, while the wife was over visiting her parents, and the health inspector came along. It was the first time he had come around since we had bought the business. He was a kind of a small man, maybe five feet, five inches, 110 pounds maybe.

I told him I was starting to build a new mobile home park and he agreed that was a good idea. We had coffee while I showed him my plans etc. Then we went out to the motel so he could inspect the rooms. While he was looking around he noticed we had "'Inn-Room" coffee makers.

He said, "Mr. Hubbell, how do you wash the coffee pot and cups?" I said, "The girls just wash them in the bathroom sink." I thought he was going to come unglued! He said, "No, you can't do that!" I said, "Yes, we do it." He said, "you can't do that unless you've got 180 degree water coming out of that hot water faucet." I said, "Yes, we've got that." He said, "No, you don't, I've been inspecting hotels and motels for twenty-five years and I've never seen 180 degree hot water in a bathroom sink!" I said, "Yes, we've got that."

He said, as he pulled a little thermometer out of his inside suit pocket, "I'll eat this thermometer if you have 180 degree hot water coming out of that faucet!" He turned on the faucet and held the thermometer under it and I was looking over his shoulder as the temperature kept coming up and up and stopped at 182degrees. I said, "Mr. Hunt, when you eat them thermometers do you like cream and sugar on them or do you just eat them plain?" He just shook it dry, put it back in his pocket, signed the inspection form, said "Good by" and left. Of course the only reason the water was so hot was because it was January or February and I had the furnace cranked up because the motel had hot water heat! Not long after though I put a tempering valve on the domestic hot water line before somebody scalded themselves and I got sued! He'd come back every couple of years and we'd always have coffee and I'd ask him if had eaten any thermometers lately and he'd just smile and shake his head.

Johnson, Peggy,
Elizabeth and Laura

I always looked forward to going to South Dakota to visit Johnson, Peggy, Evert, Edith, and all the relatives! Johnson and Peggy had moved onto Johnson's grandparents' farm just a mile north of where Johnson had grown up. I can remember helping him shovel corncobs into his furnace to heat the house! By now they had another little girl, Laura.

Some eight-ten years later, they built a nice new house.

I only drove out there a couple of times maybe. After I had gone in with Lloyd and Byron, I'd fly the "170" out

Johnson and Hubbell with " Cessna 206" on Johnson's driveway.
You can see the power pole in the background

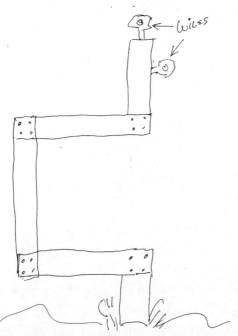

Here's a "reasonable facsimile" of the
"Modified Power Pole" drawing I had sent Johnson

there and land on the highway out front of Johnson's farm. Then I'd taxi up his driveway and park in the yard. There was a power pole about halfway up the driveway on the left side and I'd have to get the right wheel out in the ditch to get around it.

When we'd leave, Peggy would drive south to the top of the hill and Johnson would drive north in case any cars were coming, and I'd takeoff North or South depending on the wind!

When I got back home, I sent Johnson a drawing showing how he could nail on a couple of two-by-eights--each about four feet long-- on each side of the pole about four feet above ground pointing south. Then he could nail on a couple more two-by-eights--each about five feet long going straight up. Then he could nail on two more going north back to the pole. Next he could cut the pole off at the two-by-eights, creating a gap in the pole so I could pass my wing tip through it and not have to get out in the ditch. Johnson doesn't share my "if there's a will there's a way, get it done" type of attitude, so he never acted on my idea!!

Thirty some years later, in September of 1998, I was out there for Linell's funeral and we were driving out to the cemetery. Johnson's oldest daughter, Elizabeth, was sitting up front. She might have been about six or seven years old when I sent that drawing out to Johnson. She turned around and said, "Les, I still laugh when I think about that drawing you sent dad to cut the power pole off so you could fit your wing through it!"

I don't know how many other airplanes I landed on the highway and taxied into Johnson's yard. When I was selling airplanes out of Duluth, I'd often get sent out to ferry new Cessnas back from the factory in Wichita, Kansas. There were a few times that I needed to head north to get around the backside of some weather. If I ended up near Erwin and was flying a "180"or "185," I'd sometimes land on the highway in front of Johnson's farm and taxi right up into his yard for a visit or to spend the night. I'd always make a low pass before I'd land, or even if I wasn't going to land!

A couple of the times when I went out to visit Johnson and Peggy, I took my old Air Force records with me. Johnson and I would go through our orders and "remember this guy and that guy," and have some good memories and laughs!

As soon as I got my plans back from the state, I got Herbie or Dave on the end of a tape measure and we staked off the corners of the new park and brushed pathways between the stakes etc. One day while we were doing this a guy drove in and wanted to know what we were doing. I told him, and he said he sold birch fireplace wood and he'd cut all the trees down and pile the brush if he could have all the birch and other wood.

This was about the first of June so I said "Can you have it done by the end of June?" He said he could, so I said, "You've got yourself some birch wood, go for it!" And he did exactly what he said he would. Come the end of June it was all clear cut out there and the brush was piled into maybe a dozen piles. I burned those whenever we'd get a south or southeast wind so as not to smoke out my neighbors.

While I was doing that, another pickup truck drove in. A guy got out asked, "What are you doing out here?" I told him, "I'm going to build a new trailer park." He said, "I'm in the logging business up in Ely and I've got a lot of equipment just sitting around until winter. Can I level this off for you?" I said, "Give me a quote." He walked around, went up to the top of the hill, looked around, came back, and said, $3,500 dollars. (Exactly what I had budgeted it at!) I said, "Can you have it done by the end of July?" He said he could so I said, "You've got a job; do it!"

The next day he pulled in with a D6 Caterpillar on a trailer and a young kid by the name of Ronnie Baumgartner. Ronnie spent five days on the top of that hill. He'd start out with a blade full of dirt and by the time he pushed it about 300 feet to the southwest corner, he'd have a wheelbarrow full left. The boss stopped in one day and I told him that we weren't going to be done by the end of July at this rate and he agreed. He said, "I've got a couple of dump trucks and a front end loader that I could bring down but I don't have anyone to drive the front end loader." I said "I don't have much to do until we get this leveled off so I'll run the front end loader and Ronnie can go from truck to truck dumping them." He thought that was a great idea and the next day he shows up with two dump trucks and a big front end, loader!

(He didn't ask me if I'd ever run a front end loader before, so I figured, "it's like women, if they don't ask, don't tell them," so I didn't say anything.) I conveniently keep busy doing office work until Ronnie left and then I went out and spent a couple of hours checking myself out on that, front end loader. When Ronnie showed up the next morning, he probably thought I had been born on that loader!

For the next month, I was on that loader from about eight in the morning until eight at night with about thirty minutes for lunch. I had "guesstimated' that there was about eight to ten thousand yards of dirt to be moved and I don't think I missed it by much as long as it took us.

One day, about a week after we had started, I saw this white Plymouth come bouncing across the field heading my way. The driver got out and I saw him "hightailing it" over to me. I just knew he was going to be trouble, so I didn't even throttle the loader down. He said, "What the hell are you doing out here?!" I thought I'd raise the bar a little, (I hate myself when I do this) so I said, "what the f... concern of yours is it, what the hell I'm doing out here?" (I hadn't gone to go to charm school yet.) He said, "I'm from the 49ers and you can't run this machine unless you belong to the 49ers or own the land". I said, "The hell I can't; I've been doing it for a week already! And I own the land and I'm already tired of seeing you standing on it so get the hell off it!"

He said, "How about that kid that driving the truck?" I said, "I don't know if he belongs to the 49ers or not but I'm paying him to drive a truck, not talk to you, so like I said, get off my land, now!" He said, "You've probably got some

49ers living in your trailer park, and I'll have them out here picketing you!" I said, "if they do I'll have their trailers out on the street before midnight!"

He got back in his white Plymouth and left faster than when he'd driven in. A couple of days later I saw this white Plymouth again, coming my way. This time though, he was driving slower. He got out and was walking toward me so I throttled the loader down to idle. He said, "We didn't get along too good the other day so I thought I'd come back and apologize." This was probably the first time in my life anyone has ever apologized to me, for anything, so I shut the loader off and, gracefully accepted his apology. (I thought, "The hell with charm school, I don't need it!) He asked if he could talk to Ronnie and I said, "Sure," I'll go check my mail." I thought, as I was walking away, *I can be a really nice guy, if people don't piss me off to start with!* Ronnie had seen the white Plymouth the first time and asked me what the deal was and I had told him. He said, "Yeah. I can't get a job unless I belong to the 49ers and I can't join the 49ers unless I've got a job!" When I came back out the guy had signed Ronnie up and back to work we went!

When we were getting close to the final grade, I got Herbie and Dave out one evening with stakes and a couple of hammers. I had picked up a set of walkie talkie' so we each had one and I got on the transit and we staked that whole area in a couple of hours. So now I knew how much more to take here and how much to leave there! It was starting to take shape and looking good!

My friend Herb Evers, who was half owner of Lakeland Oil Company, with Howard Sunnarborg, stopped in to visit one day and to see how the new park was coming along. He said he'd put in an underground fuel oil system if I wanted to. That sounded OK to me so he decided to order a ten thousand gallon tank and supply tower and meters for each lot. I said I'd dig the hole for the tank and trenches for the lines if he'd do the installation. We had a deal!

Soon I was going to need a backhoe to do the trenching with so I started watching the paper and checking with Cool's Implement down the street a ways. Jerry Cool was a John Deere dealer and had a lot of tractors but nothing with a backhoe on it. One day I saw one in the Duluth paper and called on it. It was a Ford 8N with a Sherman backhoe on it. The seller wanted $1,800 for it. I thought, "It can't be much for that price." It was up in Duluth and I wasn't sure if I wanted to waste time to go look at it. But, my older brother lived in that area so at least I could visit him. That way it wouldn't be a totally wasted trip.

So I drove up to the address where they had told me the backhoe was at. I parked out front and walked around to the back of the house. A lady was working in her garden, with her back to me. I said, "Is this where the backhoe is?" She turned around and I thought she was going to faint, the way she looked at me. I said, "I'm sorry if I scared you." She said, "No it's not that." I said, "What is it then?" She said, "You look and sound just like my son-in-law." I said, "Is that good or bad?' She said, "No, that's good."

She said, "I'll go call my husband to come home and show you the backhoe." I said, "No, don't bother him, just show it to me." "No," she insisted, "He's only five minutes away and will want to show it to you himself." "How about a cup of coffee while we wait?"

So she went in a got us each a cup of coffee and we sat at the patio table until her husband came home. He did a double take when he saw me too! ("Hmmm, I wonder if I could have passed for the son-in-law with the daughter in the dark, now that I think of it?") Back then I was happily married and dedicated to my family so the thought wouldn't have crossed my mind then.

We finished our coffee and he led me out behind a shed. The backhoe was completely covered with a tarp. When he removed the tarp, I couldn't believe what I was looking at! There sat what looked like a brand new little Ford tractor with a brand new backhoe on it!

The two of them had cleaned it all up and painted it themselves. And it wasn't just a "slop it on" paint job either. They had done a really nice job. Even the tires were in good shape. He got on it and hit the starter and she just purred! He asked me if I wanted to drive it and try out the backhoe. I said "I could drive the tractor, but I've never operated a backhoe so I'll just wait until I get it home to do that, if I buy it."

We went inside and he showed me a bunch of invoices proving what had been done when he overhauled the engine and other work. He was a truck mechanic so I figured he probably knew what he was doing. It looked like a good buy to me, and I felt lucky to have stumbled on this little jewel so I didn't even haggle over the price, I just wrote him a check! (When I drove away, I thought, "I can be a really nice guy, when I think I'm getting a good deal!") I was proud of myself! I went and visited my brother for awhile and drove back home.

I had told the people that I had given my check to that I wasn't in a big hurry to pick the backhoe up, and I'd wait a week so they know my check was good. I could have called Ted but I didn't even know how I was going to get it the twenty-five miles from Duluth to Cloquet yet so I didn't bother Ted about it. I guess I was thinking I'd just drive it home.

A few days later a foreman for the Williams Pipeline Company checked into the motel while I was running the desk. They were laying another pipeline west of town and he had stayed with us often. I had a pool table and a ping pong top for it in the basement, and he and I had played both several times. He asked me, "What's new?" and I told him I had bought a backhoe up in Duluth near the airport. He said, "How you going to get it down here?" I said, "I'll just drive it home." He said, "Bullshit you will! There will be a truck out front at 7 o'clock in the morning to take you up there and haul it back!"

I called the people who I had bought the backhoe from. I told them that I had a chance to get it hauled home in the morning and if they wanted we could call my banker when I got there. But he said he wasn't worried about it and to come and get it. (Hmmm. I wondered if he was the dumbest guy around??) So the next morning promptly at 7:00, I heard "honk, honk, honk," and I went out and there was the biggest truck with the biggest lowboy trailer I'd ever seen! I got in and introduced my self to the driver and to Duluth we went!

We parked on the road out front and he lowered a couple of ramps. I just drove that little Ford right up them ramps and parked her in the middle of the trailer. We chained her down and headed home. I had to laugh, because that Ford backhoe looked like a little toy on that big trailer!! When the foreman came in to check out, I asked him what I owed him, and he said, "Nothing." I said, "I'll let you whip me in pool a few times to make it right with you." We had him over for steaks on the grill and a few drinks and we played pool the next time he was in.

We had that little motel, only six rooms, humming along, at about a 96 percent occupancy rate. This wasn't bad we thought, for two kids not knowing what we were doing!

Monday through Thursday were our "bread and butter" days. That's when the commercial guys are on the road and we had figured out real soon that we needed them to succeed! When someone would check in, and if I liked them,

I'd invite them to come over and play pool or ping pong if they didn't have anything else to do.

It wasn't long and when the regulars checked in, they'd say something like, "After I get something to eat, or call home, whatever, I'm going to come over and, "whip your ass in pool." I'd say something like, "you can try" or "better men that you have tried and failed."

It got where there'd be four or five guys in the basement playing pool or ping pong almost every night, Monday through Thursday! During the winter, when we'd have a blizzard blowing and snowing to beat heck, the wife or I would get on the switchboard and call over to the rooms and tell them, "You ain't going anyplace for a while, might as well come over and have some coffee and pancakes with bacon and eggs!!" I had remodeled the kitchen and made a countertop that would seat about seven people so that worked out great and we made some good friends. ("hmmm, could we have been the first motel with a free, continental breakfast?")

When our commercial guys would show up in the summer on vacation with their families, we'd still give them the commercial rate, six bucks, no extra charge for the wife or kids. And of course that's why they'd be back all winter! Also, I had poured a new sidewalk in front of the motel and installed light poles in front of each room. On the light poles I had installed an electrical outlet wired to a timer in the basement that would come on about 3A.M. And we had electrical cords plugged into them so if a person had an engine heater he could just plug it in. That way they didn't have to worry about if their car was going to start in the morning if it was 20-40 below zero, and they'd get heat out of the heater sooner too!

I remember one summer day I was mowing the grass out by the motel and three big black Buicks drove in. One guy, with a black suit on, got out of the first car and asked me, kind of gruffly , "How much are your rooms?" I said "Six bucks" and he said, "That's too much" and got back in the car. I knocked on the hood of his car as I walked by and said, " I don't know what you do, but you're making a lot more money than I am." They drove off, spinning their wheels, and I thought, "Great, stupid, get yourself shot."

Another time I had a guy drive in and come into the office. He wanted to know how much our commercial rate was. I said, "Six bucks." As he was registering, he said he was a truck driver and his truck had broken down. (Now, I've never considered myself to be real bright, but I'm thinking, ("Hmmm, I wonder were he got the car?")

About an hour later I just happened to be looking out the window and he drove up and parked in front of his room. Two women and another guy got out of the car with him and they hauled a couple of cases of beer into the room ("Hmmm, I'm wondering where he got the two women, the other guy and two cases of beer already. Hmmm, I think I smell a rat" here.")

I walked past the car down toward the trailer park and made note of the license number. I went back to the office via the back route and picked up the phone. I dialed up the police station and got hold of a classmate of mine and asked him if he could check a license number for me. He called me back ten minutes later and told me the car was registered to a guy from Proctor. I'm thinking, ("Hmmm, I wondering, why would a guy from Proctor with a truck broken down near Cloquet, be having a party with another guy and two women in my little motel in Cloquet?")

I called over to the room; one of the ladies answered. I asked if a Mr. "So and so" was there. I asked him if he would come over to the office for a minute. As he walked over I could see he was the guy who had registered. He came in and I asked him if that was his car parked over in front of his room. He said it was, so I asked if he was "So and so" or was he Mr. Smith? I mentioned that it's against the law to falsely register.

He was embarrassed and I told him, "I like to party as much as the next guy, but not at someone else's expense. The party rate is twelve bucks." He dug into his pocket and gave me another six dollars. Then I had him register under his real name and address. And I said, "When you're done partying be sure to take all your beer bottles with you."

They left in about an hour; we went out and checked the room; it was as neat as a pin; they didn't even mess up the bed! The wife cleaned up the bathroom and we rented it out again!

One Saturday night we got the wife's niece, Kay Johansen, to come over and watch the motel while we went out dancing, dining and maybe a little "drinking". (After I got back from Okinawa I didn't feel like I had to get, about half drunk, every night. Maybe just one quarter drunk now and then!) We got back about 12:30 and I asked Kay if she had rented any rooms. She said she had just rented number three to the driver of the semi truck that was parked out front. I said, "Number three was rented before we left." Number six was open, so I took the key for six and went out and knocked on the door of number three.

The truck driver opened the door about six inches, and I said, "Sir, I'm sorry to bother you but the girl at the desk has made a mistake, this room had already been rented. I said, "I have another room available so please come with me." Well, then he had to open the door wider and there was a woman standing there. Before I realized it, I said, "Don't I know you?" And she said, "Yes Les, and that's the hell of it!" Turned out I had gone to school with her! (I guess I was not only a "dumb kid", I wasn't very "tactful" either!)

Every Friday afternoon, about two o'clock, this "little old lady," I suppose she was about 50, would come in. She'd say, "Do you have a room for me Sonny?" I'd say, "Yes I do, Mom." We'd only charge her the commercial rate. I gave her the key to number six. She'd say, "We'll only be here a couple of hours and leave, so you can rent it again." "Thanks Mom," I'd say. She always wanted number six because it was on the far end of the motel. We'd just keep "number six" open for her on Fridays. About three o'clock a pickup truck from a company in Duluth would pull in and park in front of "number six". A couple of hours later they'd leave and my wife would go out and change sheets and spiff it up and we'd rent it again, if it was summer time!

We had a great group of friends! George and Helen Medich – they owned the drug store, plus had six kids! Joe and "Gina" Murphy – Joe worked at the Match Mill, "Gina" was a stay-at-home mother of four kids. Ted and Irene Micke –Ted was my banker, Irene was a stay-at-home mother of four kids. Jack and Darlene Carter--they had an appliance and TV store, and Darlene was a stay-at-home mother of three kids. Dick and Virgie Dreschler – Dick was foreman for Rheheluma Construction and Virgie was a secretary at the high school – they had four kids.

We'd get together once a month at a different house each month. The host and hostess would prepare the meal and we'd all bring our own booze. Sometimes we'd play cards, or darts, depending whose house we were at. But when we had it at our house, the girls would always visit in the living room, while us guys were down the basement playing ping pong or pool. Mostly we played ping pong. In fact, we'd play ping pong until we were wringing wet!

I had made up a Sunnyside Ping Pong trophy out of a piece of tree about six inches around and two inches high. I whittled it out and had glued in a piece of brass drain pipe that I had taken out from under my bathroom sink because it was leaking. Then I got one of them tape guns that you print out words on different colored tapes. I put "Sunnyside Ping Pong Trophy" on it. And every time we met at our house and played ping pong, I'd type out the winner's name and put it on the trophy.

The Sunnyside Ping Pong Trophy

Meanwhile, back at the trailer park, things were happening too! The first thing I did with the Ford backhoe was to dig as deep a hole as I could where the sewage lift station was going to be. I needed to go down fourteen feet, but the backhoe could only reach down ten feet, so we had to dig the last four feet by hand! I think that was the hardest part of building the whole park for me! The ground there was mostly clay and it had all these little rocks in it. You had to kick and jump on the shovel for every shovel full! And then we had to haul it up by the bucketful, one at a time. Thank God I had Herbie and Dave helping me. We worked hard and made as much fun as we could, digging that hole! They were both nice guys and willing workers! Someday I hope to be able to have a beer with them again! The last I heard, Herbie was in Texas and Dave was in Seattle working for Boeing.

Once we got the hole deep enough and an extra six inches for the floor, I called for a cement truck. We dumped a yard of cement down the hole and leveled it off from up above with a long pole. We had found a one by six board about eighteen inches long and nailed that on one end of the pole. Mostly we just padded it smooth. Nobody was ever going to see it again anyway!

Then I hired a local block layer to lay the blocks in about a five foot inside circle. He made quick work out of that. The cast iron sewer pipe had arrived, right on schedule, along with the copper water line, valves etc. The only other thing I was dreading to do was to caulk and lead all them cast iron sewer line joints!

Luckily, we had joined the "Minnesota Mobile Home Park Association." When we went to the first meeting, I was asked to stand up and introduce my wife and myself. I introduced us and said, "We recently bought Sunnyside Motel and Trailer Park, in Cloquet. You'd have thought I had committed murder, the way those people looked at me! I was "politely corrected", that these are, "Mobile Homes," not "trailer houses" anymore. And they were right, a lot of improvements had been made in the last few years. They had gone from using two by two wall studs to using two by fours. They were using better insulation, better plumbing, wiring, etc.

I met an engineer there who had designed a few "Mobile Home" parks. I told him that I was building a new one and I wasn't looking forward to leading and caulking all those joints! He told me about a new seal that was available, but not approved yet, called a "Dualtite" seal. He was planning on using them in the next park he built he said. The next day

I called down to Minneapolis and got hold of the person he said I'd have to talk to. I spent about an hour on the phone with the guy and ended up with the approval to use them! Boy, did that simplify that job!

When I bought the seals, they came with a tool for pulling the two pipes together. We had a five gallon bucket of vaseline and a handle with rags wrapped around the end. We'd lubricate the inside of the Dualtite seal and then the outside of the other pipe and then take the tool and lever them together. We only did a few of them like that, and then I thought, ("Hmmm, why don't I do this with the back hoe?")

After that I'd have Herbie and Dave in the trench putting the seals in and lubricating. Then one of them would hold the pipe in place, against the seal, the other one would put a block of wood in front of the pipe, and I'd just give it a little nudge with the backhoe bucket, until I heard it go, "thunk." Worked like a charm! After every fifth "thunk", I'd shut the backhoe off and go to the transit and we'd "set" the pipe and add a riser pipe for that lot. It was easy with the walkie talkies! Either Herbie or Dave, they would trade off, would be on the walkie talkie and holding the measuring stick and I'd tell them how much to raise the pipe up or to lower it.. The other guy would do the grunt work. When we finished there wasn't a pipe in that whole park more that an eighth inch off! We did the south side sewer line of the park first and finished that in late fall of 1964. And the little Ford tractor and backhoe had preformed very well.

Oh sure, I'd blow out a hydraulic hose now and then and I'd get mad because it was slowing me down. Or if it was raining, I'd get mad. Or if I had to take time to go to the old park and unplug a sewer line, I'd get mad. I wouldn't get mad at people (unless they pissed me off first), but I'd get mad at things. I'm a Gemini, so there's two of us I guess-- one with a temper and one without a temper.

My wife had an uncle, Lawrence Grandlund, who ran the office for one of her other uncles, Howard Johanson, who owned Johanson Electric, the company that was doing the electrical installation in the new park. So I'd get a chance to talk with Uncle Lawrence often when I was in there for something. He had seen me a few times when I was mad about something.

One day he told me that he was a Gemini too and that he used to get mad at things quite often. He said it took him years to learn that things happen, things will break, hydraulic hoses will rupture, sewers will plug, it'll rain, etc. He said that when he learned to accept that these things are going to happen and were out of his control, life was a lot more pleasant. I looked forward to my several therapy sessions with Uncle Lawrence and I learned a lot from his past experiences and wisdom. (I suppose he was fifty years old then and I was twenty-five or twenty-six.) I had never had anybody talk to me like Uncle Lawrence did, so I took his advice and he was right, life was better if you weren't half pissed off all the time over something you can't control! (Hmmm, I wonder if God had looked down and thought, that "dumb kid" needs some counseling about life, but it will have to be done indirectly or he won't listen. It was and I did.)

During the winters I'd be kept pretty busy plowing snow, taking care of problems in the park – frozen water lines, plugged sewer lines – occasionally moving a mobile home in or out, and painting motel rooms. I'd start on a room Friday morning after someone left. I'd take all the pictures and lay them on the bed, take off switch plates, mask around desks and headboards, cover the floors. I'd do whatever it took to get ready to paint. Then I'd paint the ceiling. By then the day was shot, and I'd go in and run the motel desk while the wife made supper and took care of the kids. Saturday I would paint the walls and bathroom. Sunday I'd put the switch plates back on, put the pictures back in place, clean the room up, leave the window and door open for a couple or hours to air out, and we'd rent it out again Monday! I'd do a room just about every weekend or two until I had all six of them painted!

The local Boy Scout troop had an "Aero Squadron" and I instructed ground school during the winter months. There were about ten boys in attendance every week. I can't remember who all were there, but I remember that Harry Lawrence and his two boys were always there.

Harry was the advertising sales manager for the local paper, The Pine Knot. I think I've heard that both of his boys went on to become airline pilots. Most of those boys were fifteen to seventeen years old. I could tell they weren't doing any aviation studying since the last meeting, so I got where when the class was over, I'd say, "Now go home and study what we've talked about and leave the girls alone!!" I knew that was an exercise in futility! After all, I'd been there already!!

Every once in awhile the father-in-law and I would jump into the "170" and fly over to Leech lake and spear Northerns. The first time we were going over there I called ahead to Hudle's Resort to see if they had spearing houses and if they had a road plowed straight enough for me to land on. He thought they did.

So Carl and I flew over there on a nice bright winter Sunday. It was about ten above even! We landed and found a place to get the airplane off the road so the cars and trucks could get by it. We walked up to the resort and nobody was around. We went back outside and I saw the door of a little shed open so we walked over there.

There was a man inside the shed, with his back to me. It appeared that he was looking for something. I looked in the doorway, and said, "Hi! I'm Les Hubbell. He turned around, stuck his hand out, and said, "Hi! I'm Les Hudle! We had a good laugh over that and enjoyed repeating that every time we saw each other!

We flew over there several times each winter for a few years after that. Every time I'd see him, I say, "Hi! I'm Les Hubbell" and he, of course would say, "Hi! I'm Les Hudle!" At least he and I would get a laugh out of it!

After the first couple of times we went over there and had become friends with Les Hudle, I'd call him before leaving Cloquet, and he'd go down and plow a place for me to park the "170" clear of the road. And then he'd start the wood stoves in our two favorite ice houses so they'd be warmed up when we got there! Which was nice, because the heater in the "170" was about nil! We got this automated to the point where we didn't have to walk up to the office any-more. We'd just leave him what we owed him, plus a tip for the good service, tucked away in the ice house someplace. Then he could pick it up the next time he was down there!

Every winter I'd had some trouble getting the fireplace going at home. I figured it was because of all the trees around the house so the chimney wasn't creating enough of a draft. I couldn't cut down any of those beautiful Birch trees so I'd have to come up with another idea.

We had the wife's parents coming over for Christmas dinner and of course we wanted to have the fireplace going so I was attempting to light it. I was out of kindling and thinking of chopping up the coffee table when I remembered a wooden orange crate down in the basement of the motel and used that for kindling instead! Then in my sleep, I was thinking about the fireplace lighting problem, and I came up with a solution!

The next working day I went downtown to a plumbing and heating shop and got a used fuel oil pump and motor. I mounted them on a two by six about 18 inches long and lagged screwed it to the wall by the furnace and below the fireplace. I drilled a three eighths inch hole through eighteen inches of concrete, just inside the fireplace glass doors, right in the center. Then I attached a nozzle to one end of some copper tubing, put a bending spring on it, made a nice ninety degree bend, put the other end in the hole, went down the basement and hooked it up to the pump. I then "tee'd" into the fuel oil line and caulked around the line in the fireplace with some cement in a tube. Then I wired an "on-off" switch in the bookcase next to the fireplace and wired it to the pump. I put some crunched up newspaper in the fireplace, put four or five pieces of firewood on it, lighted the newspaper and turned the switch on. "POOF" instant fire! (I thought, "I should have been a Rocket Scientist!")

Whenever we'd have company after that for awhile, I'd wait until they got here before I'd say, "Oh hum, I guess I could light the fireplace." I'd have it pre-loaded so all I'd have to do was strike a "farmers match," usually on the seat of my jeans, and light the newspaper and hit the switch. It was just like a blowtorch going. (Except I never burnt the house down!) In a few minutes the logs were burning good and I'd shut it off! Like they say, "Mothers are the necessity of inventions!"

I remember one evening we were having supper and I said to the wife, "I wonder why Bob Naylor isn't here yet." Bob sold chemicals to the paper mill and came in twice a month. He was from Wisconsin Rapids, Wisconsin and flew a Mooney to cover his territory. He'd land at Duluth and then rent a car from there to go to the mill in Duluth and then Cloquet.

I had just asked about him as we were just starting to eat. The TV in the living room was on and all of a sudden I heard them talking about an airplane landing on Highway Two north of Cloquet! I got up and went in to the living room, and there was Bob's Mooney, sitting at a service station, just nine miles north of Cloquet. About then the phone rang and it was Bob. He told me he was shooting the approach to runway nine at Duluth and had lost power. He said he broke out of the clouds at about 700 feet and there was Highway 194, right under him. And better yet the traffic was light and they moved over on the shoulder so he could land! Never "dinged" a thing! Jerry Bergman, who was a mechanic at Duluth airport, had already been over and inspected the Moony. It turned out that the carburetor heat door wasn't working and he'd gotten enough carburetor ice that he lost power! Jerry made a fix to the door and the Highway Patrol was going to block the road off and he was wondering if we were holding his room for him. I said, "you bet we are, and we'll have supper and a couple of "brandy and sevens" waiting for you too! We fed the kids and they were in bed by the time Bob arrived. We had supper with him and then he and I went down to the basement and played pool and had a few drinks. I only got about one quarter drunk though. (What could I do, Bob was stressed out and needed some company!)

I hadn't been into the motel basement for a few days and one morning I went down there, to get something. There was about two inches of sewage covering the whole floor! What a mess, not to mention stink! I got my fifty foot sewer tape and used most of that before I got to where it was plugged! It took another three hours to clean up and sanitize the basement! I didn't want to go through that again

So I studied the situation. There was a floor drain about fourteen inches across and a foot deep close to the south wall. I went down town and bought a brake light switch, and a toilet bowl float and rod, I attached the rod of the float to the brake light switch and mounted it to the inside wall of the floor drain. The telephone junction box for the switchboard was right above the floor drain on a wall. So I found a couple of empty wires, attached my "early warning device" up to them, went over to the house and found the other ends of those wires in the telephone junction box.

I had also picked up a buzzer. I mounted that buzzer on the wall right above my bed in our bedroom and wired it up. Then I went over to the motel basement and lifted the float, and the wife called on the basement phone and said, "They can probably hear it downtown!"

She wasn't as excited and proud as I was of my, "sewer backup early warning system" or "SBEWS" as we would have called it in the Air Force! (I thought, "Maybe I should have been a rocket scientist!") I never wanted to have to clean that mess up again, so it was comforting to know when I got up in the morning that the basement wasn't flooded!

It was about two months later though that I was awakened about 11:30 one night by that buzzer! Before I fumbled around and found the switch to shut it off, everyone in the house was awake!

I went out to the motel basement, put the tape in, unplugged it, and was back in bed in thirty minutes--no fuss, no mess, no sweat! ("Maybe I'm only the 300th dumbest kid in the world," I thought.) That buzzer went off a couple of times in the next year and that was it. Once in awhile when I was in the motel basement for something, I'd call over to the house to tell the wife I was going to test the buzzer. It would always work, so I figured the sewer must have "healed itself" and let it go at that!

Well the winter of 1964 finally turned into the spring of 1965 and it was time to get back to work on the new park. By the time the frost was out, we were ready to dig! It was probably about the first of May when we started. My backhoe could only get down ten feet deep and I needed to get down twelve feet next to the lift station. So I hired Jerry Anderson to come over with his big John Deere backhoe to trench out about 250 feet or so. I could take over from there with the Ford.

It was a Saturday and a raw, windy, rainy day. We were about seventy-five feet away from the lift station. I had a fourteen foot stick and was just following along behind the backhoe, making sure we were deep enough, and coming up about a inch every ten feet. I got to wondering, "Where's Joe?" I hadn't seen him for about thirty minutes or so. My first thought was, "He's OK." Besides, it was nice and warm and out of the wind and rain down there in the trench. We trenched about another ten feet and I started to worry that maybe he had fallen down in the trench we had dug last fall and couldn't get up because of his bad leg or something. Then I thought, "He's OK," Besides it was nice and warm and dry down here.

A few minutes later my conscience got the best of me and I climbed up the ladder to check on Joe. I stepped off the ladder just as the whole other side of the trench was caving in! It filled that trench about three fourths full, which meant if I had stayed down there, I'd have been dead before anybody could have gotten to me! (God must have been looking down again and thought, " There's that "dumb kid" again, first he's about to burn the match mill down, then he's sitting on the stern of the Gaffee watching the prop spin in a typhoon out in the ocean, or he's going sixty miles per hour out of control downhill pulling a trailer house, and now he's down twelve feet in the ground with no cribbing and the wall is about to cave in. I better get him out of there!")

That was another profound and traumatic moment of my life. Just looking down at where I had just come from and realizing that if my conscience hadn't gotten the best of me, I'd be dead right now! I was shaking at the thought of it. Just like I was when I got the trailer house stopped in the middle of the road on the way to DC. I went into the house and told the wife what had happened. I had her call the Holladome in Minneapolis and make reservations for the weekend and swore I wasn't going to work weekends anymore. "Life's too short I decided." But that didn't last very long because there were too many things that just had to be dealt with whether it was Saturday or Sunday – like plugged sewer lines, frozen water lines, broken water lines, no electricity and on and on.

It wasn't a month later and I was driving down highway 61 at about 7A.M, one morning. I was going down to Kettle River to help one of my younger sisters move. I was driving about fifty-five miles per hour, heading south. There was a tree line ahead and to my right, running east and west. I passed the tree line and immediately saw a blip in my rearview mirror. I looked back over my left shoulder and saw that a semi-truck had passed right behind me, doing about sixty miles an hour! He was heading east, on the other side of the tree line, so I hadn't seen him coming. He had failed to stop for the highway! If I had been a nano-second later, he would have "T-boned" me, and no doubt I would have been killed!

For some reason that didn't shake me like the other close calls I'd had. I found myself thinking, ("Hmmm, I wonder if God is trying to tell me something?") I didn't know why though. Since I'd come back from Okinawa and settled down into my marriage with my wife and kids, I had pretty much quit drinking, except for the occasional Saturday night when we'd go out dancing etc. and I was even trying to quit swearing as much as I used to. In fact, every Sunday we'd drop the kids off at Sunday school and my wife and I'd go to church even!

After church we'd go out to her folks. They had bought eighty acres about five miles southwest of town. They had a beautiful stand of pine trees near the road. They had a new house built in amongst the pines. It was a beautiful house with a step down into the family room, and two bedrooms, a nice living room and beautiful kitchen. I was glad for them because they had worked hard seven days a week in the store for years and deserved it. (The rest of the land was undeveloped and perfect for the kids to ride Carl's snowmobiles on in the winter.)

There would be about fifteen other aunts, uncles and their kids there too. They would have all brought something for a potluck dinner, and the mother-in-law had probably put a roast or ham or both in the oven before they came into church. Nobody ever went away hungry, especially not me!

After dinner I'd usually play a few games of cribbage with Carl. One Sunday though Carl was playing cribbage with Uncle Lawrence. So I laid down in a sunny spot on the family room floor and took a nap. When we were driving home I got my first hint that something was wrong with my marriage. The wife said, "My mother thinks you're bored because you took a nap on the family room floor. I said, "Did you tell her I'm working six days a week, twelve hours a day building the new mobile home park?" She said, "No, that's up to you if you want her to know that." So I said, "Then next week you and the kids can go out there and I'll go do something else."

Sunday was my only day off and I'd given up going fishing with friends, or flying by myself, or doing much of anything, except with her and the kids on Sundays so we could spend the day with her parents and other relatives.

Her mother could be kind of snippety I had learned, while I had worked in the store. It bothered me that her mother apparently didn't appreciate how hard I was working, to provide a future for her daughter and grand kids and it bothered me more that my wife didn't even support me by telling her mother how hard I was working during the week. I was totally in love with my wife and kids and I tried to forget what had happened, but it had triggered a little alarm in my memory bank.

So, after that, I started to do what I wanted to do on Sundays. I might still go to church or I might skip church and take a friend and fly out to Leech Lake fishing for the day. Or I might fly out to South Dakota and have lunch with Johnson's. I'd call ahead first to see if they wanted to have lunch in DeSmet. Then, if they did, I'd buzz their house when I got there and they'd drive down to the DeSmet Airport and pick me up and we'd go to town and have lunch. I would have landed on the highway and picked them up, but then I wouldn't have anyone to stand traffic guard!

I'd fly Herbie and Dave down to Solon Springs for lunch occasionally too. Once in awhile, I'd go to the in-laws, but not every Sunday, like I used to. In the winter I'd take friends and fly up north of Two Harbors and look at the moose!

One Sunday I flew up there, with my friend Don Bronikowski so he could get some moose pictures. I saw a cow lying down, and the bull moose standing by her, out my side of the airplane as we were circling. I went into a right turn so as to put them on Don's side of the airplane so he could get them on his 8mm movie camera. I was only about 200 feet in the air and when I made the right turn I saw a young bull down in the brush a few hundred feet away. So I put the 170 into a right slip so Don could film him.

I slipped down toward him and we got closer, maybe a 100 feet away and 50 feet in the air. He came up on his hind legs and was clawing the air for us! I think he was pissed at this hornet in the air buzzing him! I'm sure if we had ended up in the brush, he'd have been over there and stomped that 170 into the size of a sardine can! Then we went back and Don got the cow and bull on film too!

It was a beautiful flight up the North Shore to Grand Marais, either in the summer or winter. I'd stop to have lunch at the old log restaurant right on the Grand Marais airport. And once in awhile I'd take someone and fly down to Telemark in Wisconsin for lunch. I'd put eight to ten hours a month on the 170. Doctors Lloyd and Byron were great partners in the airplane. We just had a couple simple rules: If you went to the airport and the plane was in the hangar, it was yours. If you called the other guys first, to reserve the airplane for a future date, it was yours.

There was only once that I called Lloyd and said, "Lloyd, I'm going to fly my Dad over to my sister's in Grand Rapids, Michigan next weekend" "I don't have any plans," he said. I called Byron, "Hey, Byron, I'm going to fly my Dad over to my sister's in Grand Rapids, Michigan, next weekend." He said, "Gee Les, I've got next weekend off and I was going to call you but I've been so busy." I said, "No problem Byron, I'll go the following weekend, she's yours."

One nice thing about being self-employed most of the time, barring a plugged sewer, broken water line etc., etc., at least I could do what I wanted to do when I wanted to. Once a month we'd have an airplane meeting always at Lloyd's or Byron's, because those poor guys were always "on call." I don't think there was ever a time we met that one of them didn't get a call and have to go up to the hospital and deliver a baby or take care of some emergency!

We'd meet to pay our thirty dollars a month for the fixed expenses and six bucks an hour for flying time. We had a good relationship with each other and with the airplane. They were both great guys!

I remember, after we had our fourth child, I decided to get "neutered" so to speak. Lloyd was performing that little operation for me. As he was snipping away, he said, "I've always hoped, someday I could get even with you for flying the 170 so much!"

When we bought Sunnyside, it came with a four wheel drive Jeep pickup truck and snowplow. I think it was about a

1947 or 1948 model. I took the "flathead six" out of it and put in a "Chevy six" in the second year I had it.

But, after the winter of 1964 I had gotten tired of getting out and pulling a pin and swinging the snowplow one way or the other. So I decided to get something newer with a "hydra-turn plow" on before the next winter!

I was watching the Duluth paper and about in August, I saw the GMC dealer in west Duluth had a 1964 GMC complete with a hydra-turn. I called him but he had already sold it! I thought. "Ah shit!" But, he had another one coming in on trade soon he said. He told me about it. It was also a 1964 and it had fewer miles on it than the other one. It also had a hydra-turn plow plus a Breeden, 8000lb electric winch on it!

It was just what I wanted, so I said, "When you get it in, call me and I'll come get it!" A week later he called and I went and got a cashier's check from Ted. Herbie drove me down to Duluth. I looked the truck over. It was almost like new. It was a beautiful maroon color so I gave the guy my check and he gave me a bill of sale.

Boy, did it drive nice compared to the old Jeep! Of course it should have. It was a lot newer and had a lot more power! And did I ever like that "hydra-turn" the next winter! The heater was much better too!

The first fall I had it, I was out in our deer hunting area, hunting partridges. It had rained a lot recently and part of the tote road was under water. Well, that don't matter to us Irishmen, so I got out and turned the hubs in, putting her in four-wheel drive, and waded in. Just about right in the middle she got hung up, no traction whatsoever! I thought, ("Hmmm, might be a good time to check out the winch.")

I got out, I was almost up to my knees in mud and water. It's a good thing there was about a 100 feet of cable on the winch because I needed all it had to reach a tree. I wrapped the cable around the tree, got back in the truck, engaged the winch, and it pulled that truck to high ground--no sweat! I almost kissed that winch when I got out!

It wasn't very long and the wife was saying, "You got a nice truck. Now when am I going to get a nicer car?" (I hate it when women whine like that!)

I told her I thought she should just be "thankful that I'm letting her sleep with me and not worry about a nicer car!" Well, that little remark got me a few more nights of the cold shoulder treatment!

A few days later I was walking by her car and thought, "This car's getting a little rusty. (I was getting a little rusty too!) Maybe the wife should have a nicer car.

"So I called Doug Mathers who owned the Ford dealership downtown. I said, "Doug, my wife needs a nicer car and quick! What have you got?" He told me about a two-door, '64 Ford Fairlane he'd just taken in trade--it had only 4,500 miles on it--for only 4,500 bucks!

I said, "I'll be right down!" It was kind of bronze with a black top and a black interior. "Very pretty," I thought. It had a V8 engine with an automatic shift and it was like new in and out. He let me drive it up the hill to show it to the wife. She liked it and thought the two-door would be safer for the kids so I grabbed a check and went down and paid Doug for it. That night she was a little more considerate of my animal instincts.

Of course she probably hadn't forgotten the Saturday night, not too long before, that we came home from dancing and drinking. We weren't feeling any pain and when we got back home and in the bedroom, she took her clothes off and got in bed, and said, "Hubbell, make me feel like a woman!" So I took my shirt off and threw it at her and said, "OK, iron my shirt!" Back to the cold shoulder treatment!

It wasn't a month later and I was driving the Fairlane downtown for something. I was halfway down the

Sunnyside hill and had to stop behind three other cars waiting for the first car to turn left up to the hospital. There was a café and service station off to the left. Irene ran the café and Norm ran the gas station.

I glanced in my mirror and here comes Norm's wife Joyce down the hill behind me. She's doing about thirty miles an hour and looking to the left to see what Norm's doing and she ain't going to stop! I can't get out of her way to the left because of the cars coming up the hill, and I can't get out to the right because I'm a little too close behind the car in front of me! So I just press harder on the brakes and brace myself! Joyce turns around, about twenty feet from me and hits her brakes but still "rear-ends" me! (I've never forgotten.) She gets out and says, " Les, what did you do?!" I said, "What the hell do you mean, what did I do?!" I said, "I seen you looking for Norm over there!" We were friends so we ended up laughing about it. I couldn't help thinking later though, "I'll bet Norm never wins an argument with her with reasoning like that!" I also thought, ("Hmmm, I wonder if Norm ever gets the cold shoulder treatment?")

I still had a mobile home park to get built and was still working from 8A.M. to 8 P.M. I was digging the north sewer line and was about halfway down when I came across a boulder that the was too large for the backhoe to lift out of the way. I figured Jerry's big John Deere couldn't move it either so I didn't even call him. It was about five feet in diameter and I wasn't sure how deep it was in the ground.

I went over to Cool's Implement to see if Jerry Cool had anything to get it out with. He didn't but he gave me the name and number of an old guy who used to dynamite boulders etc. for road construction. I called him up and told him what I had and asked if he could "blow it out of the way for me." Boy, did he get excited. It must have been awhile since he'd "blown anything up," because he arrived within fifteen minutes with two sticks of dynamite in his hand! He was like a kid in the candy store!

I thought he'd poke a hole underneath the rock to put the dynamite in but instead he had me get him a little water in a bucket. Then he found some clay soil and laid a couple sticks of dynamite on top of the rock and "mudded it in." He had me move the backhoe and everybody back about three hundred feet and he lit the fuse. When that dynamite went off there were good size pieces of rock flying fifty feet in the air. I looked at that old guy, and he was grinning and drooling, he was so happy to have blown that rock apart! I asked him what I owed him. He said, "Nothing, call me again if you run into another one!"

We finished that sewer line the next few days and started on the water line. I had decided to install a copper waterline all the way from the motel to the valve that would be under the mobile home. I had told that to the engineer I had met at the mobile home park association-- the one who had told me about the dualtite sewer pipe seals. He said I'd save a couple thousand by using plastic, and I agreed. But I said, "I'll sleep better when we get one of those extremely low temperature winters with little or no snow and the frost goes down eight to ten feet. At least, if I have to, I can keep a welder running on the line all winter to keep it from freezing.

I probably would have never had to do that, but when us "Irishmen" decide what we're going to do, we do it our way. I wonder, if that's what God wants to talk to me about? (Hmmm, maybe I shouldn't be telling the wife, "It's my way or the highway around here!") Sometime people would ask me what nationality I am. I'd tell them I'm English, Irish, Dutch and Scotch. I'd say, the English, gives me my fine "mannerisms", the Irish give me a touch of "mischievous-ness", the Dutch gives me my "cleanliness", and the Scotch is "on the rocks!"

The water line went in pretty smoothly. The copper was in fifty foot rolls so I dug while Herbie and Dave rolled the copper tubing out behind me. Then one of them would take the John Deere crawler that I had rented from Jerry Cool, and, fill the ditch back up! I always had trouble with the curb stop water shutoffs in the old park. They would fill in with sand so half the time you couldn't shut them off or else they'd leak etc.

So I had decided to use four pieces of four foot wide culvert stock, each piece ten feet long, for water line manifold valve manholes. I had covers made for them with four, three quarter inch bolts, to lock the covers to the culverts so nobody would ever fall in one. And I bolted a ladder inside them so when you wanted to shut the water service off for a lot, you just took the cover, off, climbed down, shut the valve off, removed the drain cap, opened the valve under the mobile home and let it drain back. Piece of cake!

I had made up the manifolds out of galvanized pipe and had all eight valves already installed on it. So when we got to where the manhole" was supposed to be, we'd install the manifold assembly in the line and keep rolling the two inch copper away from it about twenty feet. And then I'd lift a section of the culvert with the backhoe, center it in place over the manifold valve assembly and set it down. We had cut out a section on each side for the pipes to pass through so it set down about twelve inches below the level of the water line. We installed the whole water system in three weeks. Might have done it in two if we hadn't gotten rained out for a few days!

When I was installing the sewer line I might end up leaving "thirty feet or so" of trench open all night. Well, if it rained that night, I might have "thirty feet or so" of trench with a foot or more of water in it. Then I'd have to get a pump and pump it out. Then we would be working in the mud and I'd be "pissed off" because it had rained! I think I did that twice and finally I figured out, if I've got any open trench left when we're done for the day, "Just take the cat and, fill it in, dummy!" Once a trench had been dug, I could re-dig thirty feet of it in about twenty minutes! This was a lot easier than pumping and working in the mud!

After the sewer and water systems were installed I buried the fuel oil tank and dug the trenches so Herb could install the oil system. Then I called MP&L, (Minnesota Power and Light) and they came up and set four poles in place for the electrical boxes and services to each lot. I think the whole electrical system was installed in another week.

I had bought some used boiler pipe to make the outside light post and mailbox holders out of. I spent a lot of time on a grinder, cleaning them up and welding the mailbox holders on them, and then painting them. Most of that I did in the back yard when I couldn't do anything else for one reason or another. I could turn out three or four a day. So ten days probably got that job done.

Uncle Wayne had made me a bucket, six inches wide, for use on the backhoe to dig the electrical and oil lines with. I could dig four lots, forty feet wide and eighteen inches deep, in about an hour. We laid all the wiring, installed sixteen posts--one per lot, down each side, and one in front of lot thirty-three, and installed the lights in five days. I couldn't wait for it to get dark so I could turn them on! It was a beautiful sight! I walked around the park for a couple of hours, just admiring them! And I'd think, "Just imagine, two years ago this was all woods, and look at it now!" It was starting to get too cold so we "shut down for the winter of 1965."

The house only had two bedrooms and we had the two boys and two girls all sleeping in one little bedroom. So, we decided to turn the back porch into a boys room before it got too cold! The porch was about eight feet wide and about eighteen feet long. Allowing for a four foot wide hallway to the back door, it would still make a fair size room. The outside wall was all glass windows, so I removed those, and framed in the wall and sided it, before it got cold! Then, I wired and insulated it, put paneling on, hooked up the electric heat, put a door in, trimmed it out, put some carpet down, and we had a boys room! I think I had it done in three weeks!

One evening I was on duty at the motel desk while the wife was making supper. A lady came in and was inquiring about the rooms. I was talking to her, when my youngest daughter, who was maybe, three years old, toddled over and took a look at this lady's derriere and said, "You got a fat butt." I found myself thinking, "Well, kiss renting this room goodbye," but the lady said, "Out of the mouths of babies comes the truth," and she laughed and picked LeeAnn up and hugged her.

I couldn't believe the number of people that would ring the door bell at 1:00-2:00-3:00 in the morning to ask if had a room available even when the "no vacancy" was on! And then ask me to call around to find a room for them! I'd be as polite as I could, but I've got to admit, after I'd worked hard all day and was planning on working hard and long the next day, I wasn't real happy to help someone that's too stupid too plan ahead a little and make reservations or start looking for a room earlier!

Waking me up to a ringing doorbell, at 1-3 A.M. was about the same as waking a sleeping Grizzly bear up! I would never ring anybody's doorbell at 1-3 A.M.! And if I won't do it, I can't imagine anyone else doing it! I didn't feel obligated to be their travel agent at that time of the night either! I'd tell them everything in town was filled up by 4 P.M. and that they should have stopped by at 2:00 in the afternoon or made reservations ahead during the summer months. I solved that problem too! I installed a switch so I could shut the doorbell off after we were full! And for good measure, I'd shut the porch light off too!

We must not have been filled up one night, because I was woke up, about 6 AM., by the door bell ringing steady and by someone banging on the door! I put my robe on and headed for the door thinking, "I'm going to kill this son of a bitch! I got to the door and it was a lady from the park telling me that one of my mobile homes was on fire!

I called the fire department, jumped into my pants and boots, and ran down there! There were a few people standing around and flames were coming out of a couple of windows! I knew there was a couple in there with two kids and I was going in to get them!

I was up on the steps with my hand on the door handle, ready to open it, when someone hollered at me, "Les, they're in the motel! They're not in there!" About then the fire trucks got there and put the fire out. The Fire Chief told me he could tell where the fire had started. He said, "What's on the inside of the wall, right here?" I said, "A closet." He said, "That's where the fire started."

The mobile home was destroyed along with the beautiful pine tree along side it. It turned out the guy renting it had gotten up early to go hunting, and had been looking for something in the closet, with a cigarette in his mouth, and something caught on fire after he left. (I thought, maybe he's the "dumbest kid" in the world.)

I had been afraid something had happened with the furnace or wiring or something, and it was my fault and would be on my conscience for the rest of my life! That thought caused me to sell the other two mobile homes as soon as the present renters moved out. I didn't want to live in fear of someone dying in one of my mobile homes, whether it was my fault or not!

Chapter Eleven

My Brother Van

Thinking about cigarettes and fire reminds me of my oldest brother, Van. Van wasn't as lucky in life as I have been. He was about four years older than me. I remember helping him, one Saturday, wash his Model A. I still remember being in it, sweeping it out with a whisk broom while he was checking the oil. Then I helped him adjust the mechanical brakes. After we were done with all that, he let me drive it around the hay field, with him in the right seat! Boy, did I think I was getting big! I can still hear how that Model A engine sounded while I was driving it and I thought, " I can't wait, to grow up and get a car!"

It wasn't very long after that when Van died. I can remember thinking, "He lived quite a while." I was in the eighth grade and high school seniors seemed very old to me then. Now I look at seniors and wonder how most of them find their way home in the dark.

It was years later before my Dad told me what had happened. He told me Van would get out of school in the afternoon for "OJT" (On the Job Training) and go to work down at the Stock Motor Company. He was a "gofor" ("go for" this "go for" that). My Dad said Van had filled a pickup truck with gas. The gas tank was behind the front seat, and probably not vented back then, and the gasoline nozzles didn't have the automatic shut-offs like they all have now either. My dad had determined that Van had filled the truck with gas and some of it had probably "burped" out onto his coveralls. He'd gotten in and driven away to "gofor" something and a few blocks away, he must have lit a cigarette and his coveralls caught on fire. My Dad told me Van was rolling on the ground and a guy came along and got a blanket over him and then got him up to the Raiter Hospital a few blocks away.

Can you image the fear that poor kid was feeling when he was on fire and rolling around on the ground! I can. I know the fear that I was feeling when I was sure that trailer house was going to push us off the road and we'd be going down into the trees and all three of us were going to be killed. I have tears in my eyes as I'm typing this fifty-two years later, thinking about my poor brother Van. My Dad told me he didn't know Van smoked. I don't remember seeing him with a cigarette either.

One of my most prized possessions hangs on my dining room wall. It is a picture of Van and me standing next to each other out at the farm west of Cloquet. And this book is dedicated to, my brother Van.

In the mid-seventies I was at a wedding dance for a young couple out at Central Hall, five or six miles southwest of Cloquet..I was walking along the dance floor. A lady, sitting there said, "You're one of the Hubbell boys, aren't you?" I said, "Yes, I'm Les Hubbell." She said, "I knew your brother Van; we were thinking of getting married." I said, "I bet you were the girl he had a date with, the day I helped him wash and clean his model A. She said, "Yes, I am."

I wish I had sat down and learned more about her and my brother. I can imagine that she had cried for days, maybe weeks, over the loss of her friend and future husband. I wonder what kind of marriage they would have had, how many kids, what would Van have done for a living? That poor kid, he died fifteen days short of being seventeen years old. If that lady ever reads this book, I'd still like to talk with her about my brother Van.

I'm sixty-five years old now and God has "saved my bacon" more times than a cat has lives. I've wondered, why me so many times? Why not Van once? Some things aren't for me to figure out, I guess.

I'm ashamed of myself for ever smoking, considering what happened to Van. And I didn't smoke until I joined the Air Force and got caught up in the "esprit de corps" and being away from home and on my own!

The tobacco companies were right there with the free cigarettes too! There would be cigarettes in our C rations even! And every holiday there would be a row of packs of cigarettes at the chow hall – a row four feet long and four packs wide, and ten packs high – of those little packs of "complementary cigarettes" five-to-a-pack, free-for-the taking!

Those tobacco companies knew what they were doing! They were getting us kids hooked at a very young age and at a very vulnerable time of our lives! I'm glad that after some years – too many actually – that I had the sense and will power to quit them. And, I'm assuming, correctly I hope, in this day and age, that cigarettes are no longer being served at any military chow halls. No longer being served to any young boys, – like I was back thcn!

Van Dean Hubbell and Leslie Virgil Hubbell

Chapter Twelve

The Mysterious Note

It's August 13, 2002, 4:30 AM. A few days ago I had needed a new notepad to keep notes on. I found one in a box that I had emptied a drawer-full of office supplies into last year. It probably had been in that desk drawer for years. (I had emptied one of my typewriter desk drawers into the box when I sold my hangar and office and moved everything home.)

In fact, I found that notepad in a drawer that I kept all kinds of things in – typewriter tapes, correction tapes (lots of them!), pens, pencils, staples, paper clips – everything but notepads. I kept my notepads over by my "normal" desk.

I had used five to six pages from this notepad already and this morning I used a page and removed it and found a note – a note that looked like it was written years ago! I had never seen it before. When I first started reading it, I thought it was from a woman I must have known in the past. But then I realized it wasn't. A strange, calming feeling came over me as I read it. It's beautifully written. I've never known anyone that I think could sit down and pen a note like this. I have read it many times. I love it. You may read it.

Letter from a Friend

I am writing to say how much I care for you and to say how much I want you to know me better.

When you awoke this morning I exploded a brilliant sunrise through your window—hoping to get your attention, but you rushed off without even noticing. Later I noticed you were walking with some friends, so I bathed you in warm sunshine and perfumed the air with nature's sweet scent, and still you didn't

notice me. As you passed by
I shouted to you in a
thunderstorm and painted
a beautiful rainbow in
the sky and you didn't
even look.

In the evening I spilled
moonlight onto your
face and sent a cool breeze
to rest you. As you slept,
I watched over you and
shared your thoughts.
But you were unaware
that I was so near.
I have chosen you and
hope you will remain
near. I am your friend
and love you very much.

Your friend

Jesus

This note is a complete mystery to me, as to when it was written in that note pad. But it is not a mystery as to who might have written it. (Hmmm, It probably was written about twenty years ago.) I say that because that's when I started enjoying the beauty of the earth and the sky and all the animals on earth. I was learning to enjoy a blizzard as well as to enjoy a beautiful summer day. I had learned to enjoy watching the animals that God put on earth along with me. I also started feeding the ducks, squirrels, pigeons, and birds in my back yard then.

It was back then that I first started really appreciating being up in an airplane and looking down at the beauty of the earth. It was back then that I first started appreciating climbing up through, 4 to 5,000 feet of clouds and breaking out into the sunshine on top, and finding myself saying, "Thank you God, for letting me do this!" I've often thought, "What do people do, that don't fly?"

It was back in 1978, as I was out deer hunting with the group, that I saw a deer about seventy-five feet out in the brush and shot it. When I got out there, I saw that it was a beautiful doe. She was lying upright with her legs tucked under her, looking at me and going, "blah, blah, blah." Her eyes were big and brown. I had to put her out of her misery, so I did, but it made me sick. I quit deer hunting, then and there. In fact I gave away my 30-30 Winchester, and haven't hunted deer since.

I have no problem pheasant hunting or fishing though. And I'm not saying deer hunting is wrong in any way. I believe God put animals on earth for food for man. It just wasn't right for me anymore. I had shot thirteen deer and one bear. That bearskin hangs on a wall in my back porch along with a rack off a ten point buck. I've had more fun since, just watching the deer down at Lake Maria State Park about twenty-five miles south and east of St. Cloud. I can spend hours hiking or snowshoeing out there, watching the deer, turkeys, squirrels, one black bear and one wolf!

Sometimes I wonder if I wasn't a deer in one of my past lives even! I say that because I can lie down on a grassy hill or just about anyplace out in the woods in Lake Maria State Park, and in a few minutes of listening to the wind in the trees, the squirrels "bitching" at me to move along, the crows cawing, the falling branches on a windy day etc and fall fast asleep, in three or four minutes, and sleep deep for thirty or forty-five minutes! Now days though, I have to be concerned with Lyme's disease. So I probably won't be sleeping on the ground as much as I would like to, at least in the summer.

Chapter Thirteen

Finishing Sunnyside Mobile Home Park

The winter of 1966-67 was time to paint the rooms again! Same old thing, take them all apart on Friday, paint them on Saturday, put them back together on Sunday. Repeat six times over the winter until all six rooms are done! I got where I hated painting, Well, I guess I really don't hate anything, but if I did hate anything, I'd hate painting!

I tried figuring out a way to get the wife to do the painting, but she was already very busy taking care of four kids, cleaning rooms, keeping the house clean, making meals, watching the motel desk, doing the grocery shopping, etc. I had heard though, if you want something done get a busy person to do it!

Every time I'd suggest that maybe she should paint the rooms though, I'd get the cold shoulder that night! I even tried to make her feel really important and that she was fully in charge of the motel and thus, also responsible for doing the painting, and I was in charge of the trailer park, which include fixing broken water pipes, unplugging sewers, plowing snow, moving trailers in and out, mowing the grass etc. That only got me a few more nights of the cold shoulder treatment! At least I learned that I liked painting better than not getting any loving!

In October, I put in approximately twenty-three hours in the 170. I made a trip to Chicago, spent the night, and came back. I made another one to Fargo and spent the night and back. And, of course, I made a couple of trips to Solon

Springs for lunch etc., went over to Green Bay and back one day. In December the father-in-law and I flew over to Leech Lake for fish-spearing a couple of times. I also had a lot of fun just flying around looking at deer and flying up the north shore looking at moose.

The middle of January 1967, Carl and I flew back over to Leech Lake spearing again. I remember it was cold, damn cold! The only way you could tell the heater was on in the 170 was because every once in awhile you could smell smoke as a drop of oil would hit the muffler! We had brought a heavy comforter and that felt good on the legs but my feet still froze! I was stomping my feet up and down on the floor to keep some blood circulating in them! I was never so glad to get out of an airplane in my life as when we landed back in Cloquet!

In February, I started working on the commercial pilot rating. Ray Peltier from Cloquet was my instructor. I liked Ray; he was pretty laid back; nothing too much bothered him. Of course, if he had flown with me when I first got that 170 and before I had tamed it, he wouldn't have been so laid back!

On March 9, I flew out to Erwin and had lunch with Johnson and Peggy. I hadn't made it out there for pheasant hunting in October because I needed to get as much done in the Park as I could before cold weather set in so it was time for a visit! Mostly I used the month of March for working on the commercial rating, doing eights, pylons, spirals, stalls, whatever! I flew alot with Ray and Arnie Odegard.

All of April and the first half of May I spent doing commercial maneuvers and hauling "class five" from a gravel pit about six miles north on Highway 33. I needed to fill a couple of soft spots and build up the north roadbed in the new park. I passed the commercial check ride with Ray Wallberg, up in Duluth, on May 16, 1967! I had thought maybe it was just, "dumb luck" that I had passed the private license test, but now I passed the commercial too! Maybe, I thought, I'm only the 350th "dumbest kid" in the world!

I had bought a 1948 Dodge dump truck to haul "class five" with. When I first started hauling with it, I had serious doubts about whether it would even make the first round trip or not! It had two transmissions in it. When I'd wade into the mud with it and both those transmissions were in low, it would just crawl through that mud, axle deep, idling!

I had started hauling while there was still some frost in the ground so I never got stuck even! It would take me an hour to make a round trip to the gravel pit and back and I made eight trips a day, six days a week, for about two weeks. I'd have to put a couple quarts of oil in her after lunch and again in the morning, but she just kept going. I never had any problems at all with that old truck. I didn't spend a dime fixing anything on her – just kept putting in gas and adding oil! I figured that old truck just liked me! I also figured, "She don't have enough power to hurt herself!" Thank God, she had two transmissions though!

I finally got the roads up to the grade I wanted them at .I had hired a half dozen kids to rake the bigger rocks off the lots and level the ground as needed so the sod could be laid. Every time I'd look out there though, there was this chubby kid leaning on the rake. So "one time too many" and I stopped the truck and walked over to him. I said, "If you're going to use that rake to rake up rocks, I'm paying you $1.50 a hour, but if you're just going to lean on my rake, I charge a $1.50 a hour for that." He got to work.

A couple of days later a semi-truck full of sod arrived. We all pitched in, Herbie, Dave, those kids, a couple of guys from the sod company and me. We made fun work out of it and laid all the sod in three or four days! Boy, was it looking nice now!

It looked so nice with the sod down and the lights on at night that I just was going to have to blacktop the streets to finish it off! I was going to wait a couple of years, but decided to get it done now, so people wouldn't be driving in the mud. I only had one little problem though. I didn't have the $10,000 that it was going to cost to do it! Well, I figured, "That's what they made banks for!"

So I went back down and talked to Jerry at City National Bank! Jerry figured he was extended out as much as he dared, considering the examiners etc. So I called Ted and asked him to ask Mac if he wanted my business back. Surprisingly, Mac wanted to come up and see what I had done since I had been there to see him.

The next day Mac and Hugh Toland, the vice president of the bank, came up. First I took them out and showed them the motel rooms and the furniture I had built; then I took then out to the new park, even turned the lights on – all thirty-three of them! Then I brought them into the house and showed them the kitchen, bedroom, and china closet that I had built. I showed them my "fireplace lighter" too! I didn't think they'd be to interested in my SBEWS, (Sewer Backup Early Warning System) as I called it, so I didn't bother demonstrating to them how nice that worked!

The wife spread out some financials, motel occupancy records, cash flow and all that stuff that bankers like to see. Mac and Hugh looked the paper work over and then Mac said, "You've got the most underrated financial statement I've ever seen!" We want your business back and we'll finance the blacktop too!

A couple of days later we had the paper work done and soon the blacktop was being laid down! That didn't take but four days when they got started, to blacktop the roads and parking spaces. The wife and Joe and I walked around the park that evening with Herbie and Dave and their wives, just admiring the new park. It was beautiful! When the lights came on, I thought it was spectacular!

We moved the first mobile home (I had learned at the Mobile Home Association meetings, by now, that they weren't trailer houses, they are Mobile Homes) into the new park on about July 6, 1967!

One of the very first homes to go in the new park belonged to Ray Lingren and his wife. I have seen their name still on the mail box, whenever I'd take a trip down memory lane and drive around the park now and then over the years.

Last Sunday, August 11, 2002, I drove up to Cloquet to visit my nephews and their families. I also drove through the park. There was Ray sitting on his deck. I pulled over and stopped, walked up onto his deck, stuck my hand out, and said, "Ray, do you remember Les Hubbell?" He said, "I was just thinking about you a week or so ago, wondering what the hell you're doing now!" We figured out he was thirty-three years old and I was thirty when he moved in there! He and his wife have bought two new mobile homes since they moved in, and they still have the same lot as we put his first home on.

The little pine trees that I had planted, two to a lot, are now twenty-five feet high and about twelve to fourteen inches in diameter! I took a picture of Ray standing under the pines

I can't believe I'm sixty-five years old already! Ray is sixty-eight! But I've said for years, "It ain't how old you are, but how long you've got left to live and how you're living it that counts!"

Ray drove a thirty

Ray Lindgren standing under trees that were 3ft tall when I planted them!

ton truck crane for a company in Duluth until he retired. I told him I remembered that he was always the first person to pay his rent. He'd stop in three or four days ahead of time!

We'd move a house a day, six days a week, from the old park into the new park until we had them all moved in before the winter of 1967 set in. My workload had really dropped down after I closed the old park! No more broken water lines or collapsed sewer lines to deal with! I thought, "Life is getting good for a "dumb kid" off the farm!"

Actually Ray had told me that we had moved his house and a few more in before the blacktop was down. I remember that now, because we had four or five engineers who were doing something at the Paper Mill, staying in the motel five nights a week for about a month or six weeks. I'd have them over in the evening for pool and ping pong and a few drinks. (What could I do? It was business!)

One day I was moving the biggest mobile home in the old park with my 3/4 ton GMC four wheel drive pickup. It was probably a twelve by sixty footer, and I had gotten it stuck right in the middle of the road going from the old park to the new park. It had sank in the mud just about up to the frame.

I was trying to jack it up and get some grain doors under the wheels, But about all that was happening was the jacks would keep sinking down into the mud and the mobile home wasn't coming up any! And I was getting, "pissed!" Worse yet, these four or five engineers were standing around watching, pretending they had slide rules, and telling me how many balloons full of helium it would take to lift this mobile home out of the mud! I told them how much "psi" I figured it would take to shove this jack up their asses if they kept bothering me!

Finally I went over to Cool's Implement and Jerry loaned me the biggest John Deere tractor he had. I hitched it up and it pulled that mobile home out of the mud like it wasn't even back there!

Those engineers were golfers and had asked me to go golfing with them several times. But I had explained to them that only people that had no real work to do in life had time to golf! They were great guys and we both enjoyed running each other down a little bit. I told them I didn't golf, but in appreciation for all the money I had made off them, I'd take them golfing! "Where?," they asked. I said, "I'll take three of you. Draw straws or flip a coin and we'll fly up to Otis Lodge on Pokegama Lake, just west of Grand Rapids.

So the last Friday they were staying, I took three of them out to the airport, pulled the 170 out of the hangar and took off for Grand Rapids! I don't think any of them had flown in a light airplane before so this was a totally new experience for them.

When we got to Grand Rapids, I made sure I pointed out the Grand Rapids airport. I said, "There's the airport right over there, but while we're up here, I'll take you over the golf course so you can see what it looks like." They thought that was a good idea! So I flew them over Otis Lodge and circled the golf course so they could see how it was laid out!

Then I said, "What the heck, why go all the way back to the airport and rent a car and drive back out here. I think there's enough room on that fairway down there and it ain't very crowded. Hell, we'll just land right here!" They said, "Won't you get in trouble if you do that?" I said, "Who cares!" "What about the golfers down there on the fairway?" they asked. I said, "We'll just make a low pass and shag them off the fairway!" So, I made a low pass followed by a climbing left turn and then I flew out over the lake and lined up on the fairway as the golfers were moving off to the side.

These guys are saying, "You'll be going to jail, for this, Les!" I said, "I need a vacation anyway." I remember flaring out and I had just a little bit of a tailwind and the 170 was floating along and I was saying, "Come on baby, land, there's a fence coming up." Those guys were about to "crap their pants", but I knew we had plenty of room.

When we turned around and taxied back, they saw the old faded windsock and realized I had put one over on them! (I had landed there, in the past, several times for lunch.)

I tried golfing with them, but spent most of my time out in the woods looking for my ball! Finally I said, "You guys enjoy your golf game and I'll go up to the lodge and shoot the breeze with some one. After they were done golfing, I bought them dinner at the lodge and we had a nice flight back to Cloquet. It was fun that night playing pool with them and listening to them tell the other guys about landing on the golf course as Les was saying, "Come on baby land, there's a fence coming up!"

It was kind of hard for me to realize that I had worked myself out of my job! I didn't have to fix broken water lines, unplug sewers, thaw out water lines, replace fuses in the middle of the night in the old park. I didn't have to build a bedroom. I didn't even have anything left that needed inventing!

Aerial view of Sunnyside Motel and Mobile Home Court.
I built the left, 32 lot section. You can see the house and motel and
up and left was the "father-in-laws" store and his mobile home park

Chapter Fourteen

Less working, more flying!

So the winter of 1967 was the easiest I had ever had in the last seven years! I loaded up the whole family, in my six-seater 170 and we flew out to visit the Johnsons and hunt pheasants again in late October. I landed right on the highway out front and taxied up into Johnson's yard. Can't get much closer than that I always figured!

Linell liked to fly. So whenever I had my 170 or, later, my 172, out there, I'd make sure he got a chance to fly it and I gave rides to all his kids and anyone that wanted one! He had a grass strip right on the farm. Unfortunately Linell came down with some asthma problems from breathing all the dust from plowing and cultivating as well as inhaling chemicals, pollens etc. and had to give up farming. He lived in Huron for several years and whenever I was in the area after I bought my 310 in 1989 I'd land there to visit him, Lilly and the kids. Most of the time he'd be out at the airport anyway. Otherwise I'd call the house and he'd come out. He liked to fly my 310 and I liked for him to fly it. He and his family had been very good to me and that was the only way I could repay the favor.

We always had fun going to Johnson's and I've thought often "If I hadn't joined the Air Force, I'd never have met Johnson and Peggy and the entire, Johnson family!" Come to think about it, I've never asked Johnson if he's glad he joined the Air Force and met me. (Hmmm, he's probably thinking, "I wish I had joined the Navy!")

Talking about the Navy – when I was coming back home from Okinawa, I was at a airport terminal someplace, Los Angeles, I think, waiting to catch my flight to Minneapolis. I went into the bathroom to, "take a leak". I did and was heading for the door, when I heard a guy holler, "Hey, in the Navy they taught us to wash our hands after we take a leak!" I hollered back, "In the Air Force, they taught us not to piss on our hands, when we take a leak!"

The winter of '67 was relaxing for me. We'd almost always go to church on Sunday. Some times, after church, I'd go out to the in-laws. Most of the time I'd go flying, fishing, snowshoeing out in our hunting area, or visiting friends. Or I could be plowing out the mobile home park and motel too! And I also always plowed out the in-laws' grocery store and their mobile home park, which we were managing for them.

January of 1968 arrived right on schedule! It was too cold to fly much – especially with the inadequate heater in the 170. I did make a trip on the fourteenth, up north of Two Harbors with the father-in-law to look at the moose. That was always a lot of fun! They were so big and majestic. On the sixteenth I went down to Solon Springs for breakfast, with Herbie and Dave. On the twenty-first I flew out to DeSmet, South Dakota. Johnson, Peggy and their girls picked me up, and we went into DeSmet for dinner. I was getting to like all the free time I had now that the new mobile home park was done!

I remember the end of February. Byron and I flew the 170 down to Maxwell Prop Shop at Crystal Airport. We were a little concerned that maybe the prop was getting out of limits or something. I flew the 170 down there and we landed on Runway 13 and taxied to the Maxwell Prop Shop. It was much warmer in Minneapolis than it was when we left Cloquet! It must have been in the high fifties. In fact it was so nice that Maxwells had their big hangar door open!

I taxied up and parked parallel to the hangar, heading northwest, and stopped about ten feet short of the open hangar door. We went in to the office and introduced ourselves to Mariam and Jim. Jim came out and looked at the prop, took a couple of measurements and said it was OK for a while yet. We asked what we owed him and he said, nothing, just come back if you ever nick it or something.

Since I had flown down there, Byron was going to fly back to Cloquet. We got back in the 170 and Byron started her up. We were so busy trying to hear and talk to ground control on our VHT3 that we both forgot the open hangar door. We finally decided, over the noise of the engine, (this was long before intercoms) that ground wants us to taxi to Runway 13. So Byron gives her a shot of power and, as she started, to roll some right rudder and brake to taxi over to the taxiway.

All of a sudden we had a mad Kenny Maxwell knocking on Byron's window. We shut down and he "chewed our asses!" "Don't they teach you young pilots anything anymore? Etc., etc.! We just swept that hangar out and now you've blown it full of sand! I should make you get out and sweep it!" We got out and apologized and offered to sweep the hangar out, but Kenny said, "Just get in your airplane and leave!"

He pushed the tail around so we wouldn't blow anymore sand into the hangar! That was the worst "ass chewing" I'd ever had and I've never "turned tail" to another open hangar door after that! And I bet Byron hasn't either!

After I started up L.V.H. Aircraft (Leslie V. Hubbell Aircraft) at Maple Lake, Minnesota, in August of 1982, I'd get whatever propeller and governor work I needed at Maxwells. They did both props and governors on my 310 and a few single engine props over the years for me, and I sent him any business I could. In his later years Kenny mostly just liked to re-calibrate tachometers. It seemed like about half the airplanes I bought had "tachs" which were inaccurate, so I'd take them over to Kenny to have them re-calibrated. I had gotten to know and like Kenny pretty well by now. One time he was doing "his thing" on one of my "tachs", and I was watching him. I asked him, "Kenny, have you got a single daughter?" He gave me a cold stare and said, "Why?" "Well," I said, "if you've got a single daugh-ter, I'd like to marry her so I can inherit some of your money someday!" Kenny just laughed and said, "That young Einarson kid already beat you to it!"

At the end of April, the wife and I flew the 170 down to Minneapolis for the day to attend the Minnesota Mobile Home Association Convention.

About the Middle of May 1968, Byron, Lloyd and I decided to sell the 170. As I remember we sold it to a couple of young airline pilots down around Lakeville. About the first of June I bought a 1966 Cessna 172, N4162L, that Arnie owned out at the airport. I only flew it once, down to Minneapolis and back. The next day we left for Leech Lake with Carl's tent camper hooked up to his new Ford Fairlane. (He didn't even say, "Try to not burn it up." I thought that was nice of him!) We camped out for the weekend and came back Sunday evening about 6:00.

I wasn't in the house ten minutes and the phone rang. It was Arnie calling to tell me that, "It had rained to beat hell Friday and Saturday and then the wind got strong enough to pull the tie-downs on Charlie Potter's J3 out of the ground! Charlie's J3 had become airborne and damaged the right wing on my plane as it went by! It was damaged bad enough that I had to get a new wing! I thought, "It never fails, first the Fairlane, and now the Cessna!" It didn't take long though and they had a new wing on it and painted and I was back in the air!

In the middle of June, I started the instrument course back up at Duluth Airways using their C150. I started out with Terry Anderson and Jim Nelson as my instructors. Later Carl Lucas became my full time instructor.

Chapter Fifteen

My Counselor Dies

On June 22, 1968, I had flown down to Solon Springs with Herbie and Dave for breakfast. We were halfway done eating and the waitress came over and said, "Les, you've got a phone call." I went and picked up the phone and it was the father-in-law. He told me, "Uncle Lawrence died last night in Sioux Falls, South Dakota." Then he asked me if we could fly down and pick up Aunt Cora and bring her home, when I got back. I said we'd hurry up and finish eating and I'd be back at the airport, in forty-five minutes! Uncle Lawrence liked to sing and he belonged to the "Vikings," singing group. He and Aunt Cora had gone to Sioux Falls for, as I recall, a Vikings Songfest. Uncle Lawrence had suffered a heart attack and died during the night.

We had taken my truck to the airport so I had Herbie and Dave drive that back to my house and said I'd ride back with Carl when we got back. I filled the 172 with fuel and Carl and I headed for Sioux Falls. Our flight path took us right over the town of Tracy, which had just about been wiped out by a tornado a day or two earlier. There was a path of destruction a block wide, from the northeast side of town, running right through the middle of town to the southwest, as I remember. There wasn't much of anything standing where that tornado had gone through!

We got to Sioux Falls in about two hours and forty-five minutes. Aunt Cora was waiting for us at the airport when we got there. Carl and I hugged her and tried to give her whatever comfort we could. I went out to check on the refueling and to pre-flight the airplane for the return trip to

Cloquet. I think Aunt Cora was in a state of shock and understandably so. She sat in the back seat and didn't say a word all the way home.

She and Lawrence had a very good marriage and all of a sudden "she's alone." I can't imagine the pain of that happening. One minute your loved one is there, the next minute, gone. I had just turned thirty-one years old five days earlier, so I'd guess Uncle Lawrence and Aunt Cora were maybe about fifty-five years old then. Not very old, as I look back now. And I didn't have Uncle Lawrence to talk to anymore. I've always appreciated and never forgotten the counseling I got from him.

Jerry Cool called me one day and asked me if I could and would, fly him and Mrs. Cool to Platte, South Dakota and back in a day. They had a wedding in the family that they would like to go to, but couldn't be away from their business long enough to drive out there. This was my chance to repay the Cool's for the all the tractors they had let me use over the years, so I said, "Of course I could and would!"

On June 29th, the weather was "CAVU" (Clear And Visibility Unlimited) and we had a beautiful trip out to Platte, SD. We were bucking a head wind on the way out there so I landed at Montivideo for fuel. We arrived at Platte about 11:30 and I told them to take their time and enjoy the wedding and reception and not to be in any hurry. They said they'd be ready to head back in a couple of hours.

I caught a ride into town with the people who picked them up and had lunch. Then I walked back out to the airport and got the 172 re-fueled and ready for the return trip. Just about two hours and fifteen minutes after we had landed, the Cools were back and we loaded up and took off for Cloquet. The weather was still "CAVU" and not a bump even! Now we had a nice tailwind on the way back so we made it non-stop to Cloquet! I was glad I had a chance to "give back" to the Cools for them being so helpful to me when I needed it!

Chapter Sixteen

Flying for Northland Homes

Dave Goldberg, President of Northland Homes, who had put several homes in our mobile home park over the years, called and wanted to know if I could fly him down and back to River Falls, Wisconsin. He had to attend a meeting. I did that and soon he was calling to go to Eau Claire, Shawano, Stevens Point, and Marshfield in Wisconsin, and to Brainerd, St. Cloud and Grand Rapids in Minnesota where the company had mobile home sales lots. I worked out a lease with Northland Homes for them to use the airplane with me as their pilot. Pretty soon I had a full time job just flying Dave, Bud Sailors, the Vice President, and managers around the upper midwest!

I spent most of July, August and September and the first week of October working on the instrument rating with a trip now and then with Northland Homes. I passed my instrument check ride with Ray Wallberg, on October 6, 1968! I thought, ("Hmmm, maybe I'm only the 400th "dumbest kid" in the world!")

On October 8th I flew Dave to St. Paul for a meeting and then we went over to Stevens Point, Wisconsin where he had another meeting and I then dropped him back off at Duluth and flew back to Cloquet. Dave had been driving to all these places for a couple of years so he really liked being able to hit all his sales centers and be back home in two days! On October 10th I flew Dave down to Guttenberg, Iowa. I like landing there. The grass runway was in the middle of a peninsula, surrounded by houses, with no overrun on either end.

On October 19th I took Ted Micke and one of his boys and my oldest son Tim and we flew out to Lake Preston South Dakota to pheasant hunt and visit with Johnsons. Lake Preston is about twenty miles from Erwin, so Johnson and Evert drove down and picked us up.

We hunted down at Linell's and as usual the hunting and

Evert looking over "62Lima

eating were fantastic!

On October 28th I flew Herb Evers up to Ironwood, Michigan so he could look at a car wash that he was considering installing at his service station.

I was really enjoying all the flying I was doing! It was still hard for me to believe that I didn't have to work six days a week, twelve hours a day anymore! Mostly all I had to do now was the normal, fixing in and around the motel and house and mow the grass! On November 27th Bob Naylor needed to go to Brainerd so he could call on the paper mill there. His Mooney was parked up in Duluth. So rather than have him drive to Duluth, get in his Mooney and fly over Cloquet to get to Brainerd, I said, "Come on, I'll give you a ride in a real airplane!" So we took the "172" and flew over to Brainerd.

Once in a while Arnie would call me from the airport and need me to fly someone from the paper mill in Cloquet, over to Brainerd to the paper mill over here. It was about a forty or forty-five minute flight with about a two hour lay over and the return flight. If I had time, I'd do it.(and most of the time, I found the time!)

He had a 1968 Cardinal, the first year Cessna made them, with the 150 hp engine. In 1969, Cessna put a 180 hp engine in it, making it a little better performer. I didn't think there was really anything wrong with the 150 horse. I just treated it like I did the wife, "Don't demand too much, and she'll do her thing when she's damn good and ready, not a minute or a foot sooner!"

In December, Dave told me that if we had a twin engine airplane, we'd go farther and more often. So we drew up another lease and I started looking at twins. Arnie didn't have a twin to give multi-ratings in so he told me to call Thunderbird Aviation down at Flying Cloud Airport in Minneapolis and talk to Don Huseth.

I called and talked to Don about needing a multi-rating and he told me they had a twin Comanche that they used for that and he'd be ready when I was.

So I flew the 172 down to Thunderbird on January 10, 1969 and met Don. We spend a couple hours or so reading the manual and talking about flying twins and went out and pre-flighted, N8626 Yankee. We flew an hour on the tenth, 3.7 hours on the eleventh, 1.3 hours on the twelfth, 1.9 hours on the morning of the thirteenth for a total of about eight hours and Don signed me off. After lunch I took the checkride which lasted "point.9" hours, passed it, got in the 172 and was home 1.6 hours later for supper! I thought, as I was flying back to Cloquet, ("Hmmm, maybe I'm only the 450th dumbest kid in the world!")

I made a trip back over to Brainerd in Arnie's Cardinal on the seventeenth of January. I spent the rest of the month flying for Northland Homes along with doing the usual work of snow-plowing the motel and mobile home park. And then I'd plow the father-in-law's store and mobile home park. When I got done with that I'd run the motel office and watch the kids, so the wife could get out of the house to go shopping or visiting once in awhile too!

I made a couple of trips to Minneapolis, looking at twins, in February and about six trips with Northland Homes to Guttenberg, Stevens Point, Marshfield, Mankato, and St. Cloud. (Little did I know that someday I'd live in St Cloud!) St. Cloud built a new airport out east of town in about 1975. When I fly over the town now, I can look down at the site of the old airport and still see parts of the old runway. It now comprises the Whitney Senior Center and a few baseball diamonds and a park area.)

Also in February, a guy stopped in one day and wanted to know if we wanted to sell the motel and mobile home park. Until then we hadn't even thought about it. But we talked it over and we had been in the motel and mobile home park business for almost nine years. Nine years was considered the so-called "burnout time." I also considered the fact that I was having fun flying all around with Northland Homes while the wife was "saddled down" with the business.

I told Dave, on one of the flights that I had a guy interested in the motel and park and he said, "If you sell it, I'll hire you full time to be our pilot." Well, that made that decision a little easier so we sold Sunnyside Motel and Mobile Home Park sometime in late February and bought a house on the north side of Duluth, out on the Martin Road

I rented a hangar at the Duluth airport for the 172. From March 5th through the 8th Northland Homes kept me busy going to St. Cloud, Mankato, St. Paul, Marshfield, and on up to Baudette and back.

I had decided that I liked the "Twin Comanche" and thought that it would do a good job for me and Northland Homes. I had made several calls around the mid-west inquiring about different Twin Comanches and finally found one over at Green Bay Aviation, that sounded worth going to look at. So on March 13, I flew 4162Lima over there and I looked at their turbo-charged Twin Comanche with tip tanks, N8034Yankee, while they looked at 62 Lima and after a couple of hours, we made a trade. The hardest part was getting insurance! I only had 375 hours total time and 7.9 hours multi-time! That same day I flew an hour with Bob Jubin and the next day, March 14, I flew four hours with Bob again.

I still didn't have any insurance so I had to spend another night. It was after lunch before my agent got me insured with Loyds of London! I had her topped off with gas and headed back to Duluth and made a night landing. I thought, coming down final, "There's not much of anything prettier than a full IFR runway, lit up at night!"

The next morning I flew 3.9 hours, doing takeoffs and landings, single engine work, etc. around Duluth. I think I was supposed to get 25 hours solo in it before I hauled passengers, but I felt very comfortable with the airplane so that afternoon I flew Dave and Joe Bullyan and their wives to Mankato, Minneapolis and back to Duluth! With a night landing at Duluth! Again I thought, coming down final, "There's not much of anything prettier than a full IFR runway lit up at night!"

That was the first time, of course, that I flew it with four people in it and I found out "She lands a lot nicer with weight in the back seats!" (God must have looked down and thought, "There's that dumb kid again! Just gets a twin, hauling passengers already, and the first trip he's probably overloaded already!")

I liked 34Yankee right from the start! It just felt right! I flew it for Northland Homes every day through March 26! On the 17th we went to Lafayette, Indiana, stayed over night, returned to Duluth. The next day I took Bud Sailors and Bill Kuppersmith to Mankato and St. Cloud and returned to Duluth two days later. On the 25th we went to Shawano, stayed overnight and returned the next day.

I was having fun doing my new job! And every night it was steaks and "one" drink for me! The other guys would stay longer, but I'd go to my room by 8:00 and call my wife, maybe read the local paper, be in bed by nine. I figured if I was flying the next day, I needed a good night's sleep!

In April I made eight trips all around the mid-west for Northland, putting about 38 hours on 34Yankee. On May 4th and 5th, I put on 3.4 hours just doing "hood work" (practicing flying on instruments) with one of the local instructors. We went out northwest of Duluth and did some stalls, single engine work, etc. Even the instructor was impressed when he cut an engine and I just reached down and brought the Ray Jay turbo on line. You could see the vertical velocity needle come to life and the altimeter start climbing!

The last approach into Duluth was the ILS runway 9. When we landed and were rolling out the instructor said, "That was a perfect ILS, Les, I never even saw the glideslope needle move!" I said, "If you think that's good, wait until I get a glideslope receiver!

What I had done was tuned the 2nd nav to the, DLH VOR and whatever radial I had figured was about halfway between the middle marker and inner marker. I had figured, "If the outer is 3,300', the inner is 1,628'. Hmmm, that's about 1,700' difference, divided by two – 850 feet. I should be about 2,400' – halfway) So I had just kind of "interpolated" the altitude I should be at on the way down. Besides, some days you just can't beat dumb luck!

It wasn't long after though, and I had a glideslope receiver installed. The rest of May I flew for Northland, just about every day again, all around Minnesota and Wisconsin. Every night it would be steaks and "one" drink for me, and I'd be in bed by nine. On May 30th I took the family and we flew 34 Yankee out to Lake Preston, South Dakota to visit the Johnsons and came back the same day. I had gotten to really like "34 Yankee!" She turned out to be every bit as good as I'd hoped she'd be!

June of 1969 was more of the same – flying all around Minnesota and Wisconsin! On the 5th I took Dave, Harold and John to Des Moines and returned, landing back in Duluth about 8 P.M. I always drove the Airport Road to the east going home. When I stopped at the intersection of the Haines Road, there was a dog there. It was a golden lab.

I rolled the window down and said, "Where do you live?" She put her paws up on the door and looked at me with pleading brown eyes. I opened the door of my little blue '1967 Mustang and she crept in under my legs and got up and sat in the right seat. I said, "Just make yourself at home," since she already had.

It had been just a week earlier at supper when the kids had asked me if they could have a dog. I said, "OK, let's vote on it. How many kids want a dog?" Four hands went up. I said, "OK, now if we get a dog, we also have to get a shovel and a rake." "What do we need that for Dad" they asked. I said, "Because once a week you'll have to go around the yard and rake up the "dog biscuits" and throw them in the woods. I said, "Now how many kids want a dog?" Only the oldest son Timothy's hand went up.

The closest house with lights on was a quarter of a mile away so I drove over to it. I went up and knocked on the door and a lady opened the door. I told her about the dog in the car and asked her if she knew who might be the owner.

She said she didn't know who owned it but she had seen it around that intersection all afternoon. I left her my telephone number in case anyone came looking for it.

When I got home Timothy saw my car coming up the driveway and ran down to open the garage door as he always did. When he saw that dog his eyes got as big as saucers! He was all excited, "You got us a dog dad!" He couldn't wait to pet and hug that dog!

So I told him how I had found her and we'd have to put an ad in the paper to see if she was a lost dog or not. The kids were really happy to have a dog and the dog was really happy to have a family! On the tenth I took off with Dave, Bud, Dick and John heading to Green Bay, Lafayette, Elkhart and back to Marshfield for the night. We were climbing out of Duluth and Dave asked me if I could tune in one of the local radio stations so they could hear a new ad for the Duluth sales center.

Pretty soon I heard, "Lost dog in the Kenwood area" and a description that sounded like the dog I had picked up a few nights earlier. I wrote the phone number down on my flight plan.

That evening, after a steak and a drink, I called home, Timothy answered with a "Hello." I said, "What happened to "Hubbells' residence, Timothy speaking?" He said, "Oh, it's you Dad. I don't want anybody to know where the dog is."

So I chatted with him for a few minutes and then talked to the wife. I told her about the ad and gave her the telephone number to call. When I got home the next day she said she had called the number and those people had found their dog, so "we had a dog!"

About two weeks later Ginger, as we had named her, was lying on the laundry room floor giving birth to about six little puppies! Now we knew why someone had dumped her! We all loved her though and let her enjoy her puppies for a couple of months. Then we found good homes for them with friends and neighbors so she could still see them now and then!

Where ever we went, I'd always go along to the sales centers or mobile home factories with Dave and Bud, or whoever I was flying that day. All these guys were great to me! It was fun going through the factories to see how the different brands were made, etc. And, of course, every night it was steaks and drinks (but just one drink for me) and I'd call home and be sleeping by nine!

In July I was busy right up through the 18th of the month! On the 11th we stopped in Eau Claire and picked up John Menard and flew down to Guttenberg, Iowa and then over to Boone, Iowa and then brought John back to Eau Claire. I remember when I was introduced to the owner of the "manufactured housing" factory at Boone, he said, "Hubbell – that's like "Vanderbilt" down here. I asked him, "Why?" He said, "The "Hubbells" built Des Moines by bringing the railroad to town, etc. I said, "Yeah, but I'm from the other side of the tracks though. "Us Hubbells don't have a pot to piss in or a window to throw it out of hardly!"

I knew I was going to get addicted to float plane flying right from the start. On July 19, 21 and 22, I got an hour of "seaplane dual" each day. I was flying in Duluth Airways' Cessna 150/150 with instruction from Carl Lucas. On the 27th I soloed it for 2.1 hours. Was that fun! On the 28th I flew with Carl again for .6 hours. I soloed again on the 30th for 1.2 hours and again on August 1st for .9 hours.

Then I went flying with Northland Homes for a few days to Ironwood, Michigan to the Schultz factory, to Guttenberg, Iowa to Brainerd, Minnesota and to Elkhart, Indiana and back on the 8th. Every night it was steaks and drinks (just one drink for me though!) and I'd call home and be in bed by nine!

And on August 10th, I flew the 150-150 on floats with Ray Walburg. He signed my log book off to go take the seaplane checkride! I thought, ("Hmmm, maybe he's not too bright either!")

On August 16th, I flew Dave and his wife and kids over to Benton Harbor, Michigan. They were going to be staying there for the night so I flew up to Grand Rapids and spent the night visiting my oldest sister and her family. The next afternoon I flew back to Benton Harbor and picked up Dave and his family. From there we flew to Kankakee, Illinois and back to Duluth!

I loved my job flying for Northland Homes! I couldn't believe how nice and easy it was to be going from here to there, back to here, over to there, etc.! And the Twin Comanche was working out perfect for us!

On the 18th I flew John Hinks down to Mankato and back, on the 19th I took Dick Schletty to Guttenberg, and on the 20th, I flew the vice president of Northland Homes, Bud Sailors, and his wife, Mary Jane, to Sturgis, Michigan. This was home for either Bud or Mary Jane or both. They visited family there for a few hours, then we went to South Bend and picked up Dave, stopped at Kankakee for a couple of hours, and back to Duluth!

I was kept busy flying Northland people around to several sales centers and even took a trip into Chicago O'Hare on August 25th. Did we ever look small taxiing in and out with all them big jets! I was especially careful to avoid their "jet blast" during taxiing!

I flew for Northland again on the 26th and 27th so it was August 31st before I got a chance to get back together with the, "150-150" on floats! I spent a hour playing with it and the next day flew it up to Grand Rapids, Minnesota to take my checkride with the "God of seaplane flying", Gordy Newstrom. I had apparently been pretty well prepared by Carl. The checkride was more like a lesson listening to Gordy tell about some of his experiences flying floats. So I passed! I was very happy and couldn't help touching down on a couple of lakes on the way back to Duluth! I thought, ("Hmmm, maybe I'm only the 500th dumbest kid in the world!")

On September 3rd I flew Dave and two other guys down to Chicago Midway airport. They had a meeting downtown and would be spending the night there so I checked into a motel near the airport. Come to think about it, that was probably the only night that I had flown for Northland that I didn't have steaks and drinks (just one for me though!). The next day we flew over to Meigs, up to Green Bay, and back to Duluth!

It was in September that I first met Joe Sebastien. He had been hired as a district manager. Joe and I shared the same warped sense of humor and soon became friends. I remember it wasn't very long and I was flying Joe and another guy that had just been hired, over to Ironwood. The Schultz Mobile Home Factory was in Ironwood. I had been there several times already.

Going across Wisconsin, the new guy asked, "What's that town down there Les?" I looked down and said, "Damned if I know." Pretty soon he said, "What lake is that over there Les?" I looked "over there" and said, "Your guess is as good as mine?" Pretty soon the guy leans forward and whispers in Joe's ear. Joe said to me, "He said, 'If you don't know where you're at, how the f… do you know where we're going!'"

We'd had our fun so I showed him my "low chart" and said, "When these two needles get centered we will be right here. But," I said, "if you really want to know the names of those little towns and lake down there, I got another map for that!" So I dug out a sectional chart (map) for him to use, and showed him where we were at.

Dave called me into his office one day and said, "Les, with all your mobile home park experience, setting up mobile homes etc., I'd like you to handle another job for us. And I need to you give you another title to justify you to the stock holders. He asked if I'd mind being the Director of Customer Relations. Well, that sounded like a pretty fancy title for a "dumb kid" off the farm, so I asked him what it meant! He said, "You'll be in charge of all the service department personnel and it would give you something to do when we visit the sales centers." Then he gave me a raise for the extra work and I was happy! Hell, I had this flying around the country down pretty good so it was OK to take on something more! But, I got him to agree to one thing. When I was within fifty feet of the airplane, I was the pilot, not the Director of Customer Relations. I said, "I don't want anyone talking service to me when I'm flying!" He agreed and sent a memo around the office and to all the sales centers announcing my additional title and the terms of my accepting it.

I flew just about every day in September! I was getting where I knew the frequency of every VOR, unicom, center, tower, and ground control within Minnesota and Wisconsin! The few days I didn't fly I was designing a standardized check list for the set up of mobile and manufactured homes.

Now I was having fun not only flying 34 Yankee but taking care of my new responsibilities also! When we'd go to a sales center, Dave and Bud would meet with the manager and sales people, and I'd go meet with the service manager and technicians.

For once these guys had someone that went to bat for them! First I met with them and listened to what they needed – tools etc., – to do a better job. A couple of the centers needed new tow trucks, so we got a couple of new trucks.

I suggested we'd look more professional if everyone dressed more professionally. Pretty much everyone agreed with that and I got them all uniform pants and shirts with a small "Northland" emblem with their name on it.

In the past, the sales departments would earn a lot of trips from the manufacturers – trips to Hawaii and other places.

The service centers got shit! So I designed a Customer Satisfaction Survey form.

I'd send this form out to buyers after they had their mobile homes for thirty days. It rated the delivering service center on timely delivery, satisfactory set-up and hooking up of utilities, etc. It rated them on being courteous, explaining how all the appliances worked, making sure all lights worked, furnace worked etc., etc. And it rated them on how promptly service calls, if any, were answered.

The buyer could then rate everything as poor, good or excellent. I told the service managers and technicians that I would only count the excellent ratings as far as figuring the percentages. Then I met with Dave and Bud and explained my program and told them the benefits my service survey could have for the sales department. If every buyer is satisfied with the job our service department does, the word will get around every park we put a home in and the benefits will come back to the sales department! "But," I said, "in order to reward the service personnel and keep their momentum going, I need a couple of trips! I'd like to get a trip for two to Hawaii and another trip for two to Florida. The service center with the greatest percentage of excellent forms returned would win the trip to Hawaii for two. The service center with the second most excellent forms returned would win a trip to Florida for two.

It didn't take Dave and Bud long to see the benefits this could have for the whole company and they approved it on the spot! So for the next month, as we visited every sales center, I'd meet with the service department people and show the survey form. I told them about how it would be graded. I told them about the trips. They liked it! And I liked seeing them winning trips and being recognized and rewarded "for a job well done"! (The only thing I forgot to do though was finagle a trip for the Director of Customer Relations and his wife!)

On November 15th I flew Les Mayer, the company comptroller, down to Stevens Point. We spent a couple of hours there. While Les M. was meeting with the General Manager, I had a meeting with the service manager and technicians to see if they had any problems I could help them with. Problems like getting parts from a factory or getting tools – whatever. They had hired a new guy that I hadn't met yet, so I talked with him for awhile too. Before we left, Les Mayer came out and met the new guy also.

We finished what we wanted to do there and the General Manager gave us a ride back out to the airport. We took off and headed about 280 degrees over to Marshfield, about 30 miles away. I was climbing up through about 3,500 feet and Les Mayer says to me, "Les, how do you like that new guy?" I ignored him. Pretty soon a repeat, "Les, how do you like that new guy?" I ignored him again. Then he asked the third time, "Les, how do you like that new guy?"

I was about to level off anyway, so I pushed the wheel forward enough to put his head on the ceiling! He said, "I'm sorry, I'm sorry, I forgot, I get the point!" So I leveled off and started down and landed at Marshfield.

We spent the night there and had steaks and drinks with some of the people from the sales center. And, of course, Les had to tell them that he had asked me about the "new guy" over at Stevens Point, and how he got his head pinned against the ceiling for awhile. You'd have to know Les Mayer to appreciate the gyrations and hand movements he used to tell the story!

I liked Les. He was fun to be with as all of the Northland people were! And, he never asked me about anything other than flying after that if we were within fifty feet of 34 Yankee!

One day about six months after I had put the service survey into effect, I was sitting in my cubicle office. I was only about ten feet from the receptionist desk and pretty soon I heard a lady asking to speak to someone in charge, because she wasn't happy with her home or our service!

I was on the phone with someone when the receptionist came over and told me about this lady and laid a note with her name, on my desk. I told her to seat them in the conference room, and tell them that I'll be with them in a couple of minutes. (Our conference room was always about ten degrees cooler than the rest of the office for some reason.)

So when I got off the phone, I went into the conference room and the first thing the lady said to me was, "It's cold in here!" I said, "We keep it cold in here purposely for people that are hot under the collar. She kind of laughed and she kind of glared at me!

So I sat down across the conference table from them. I said, "I hear you're upset with our service department." She said, "You bet we are!" I said, " But it's not our fault!" "Well, whose fault is it then, Mr. Hubbell?" she asked. I said, "It's your fault." "What do you mean, my fault!" she said.

I said, "I sent you a service survey form a month after your home was delivered, asking you if there were any problems or anything that still needed to be attended to. I then asked you to rate our service department. I don't even have to go look in my file on you to see if you sent the form back. I know you didn't, because if you had I'd have been on the phone to our service manager up there on the hill, to see if they were awaiting a part or what was the holdup! And they would have been there and fixed everything already. I call every service center every week and go over any complaints I have received." Whereas you could call them and it might take them awhile to get back to you, because they are very busy. But when I call them, they find time to do it, unless they are waiting for a part!" And I said "They want to do it because the service center that gets the highest percentage of excellent survey forms back gets a free trip to Hawaii for two.

She said, as she dug the form out of her purse, "Is this the form?" I said, "Yes, it is ma-am. Why don't you fill it out now and I'll have the guys out to your house tomorrow if they have everything they need to finish the job. So she filled it out and when she got to the part to rate the service she said, "Well I guess it isn't their fault, Mr. Hubbell. So if you say they're going to be there tomorrow, I'll give them an excellent!" I said, "They will be there first thing in the morning."

The service people had been waiting for a couple of parts that had just come in. So they went out and took care of everything the next morning. I got a nice letter of thanks from her a few days later and of course I sent a copy of it up to the service center. with a copy to Dave and Bud., "I guess I never did need charm school!" I thought.

I don't know how I found time to do any customer relations and also fly fifty-one hours in September, but I did! (Hmmm, had Dave also heard that if you want to get something done, ask a busy person to do it?)

On October 6th 1969 I flew an hour, at night, with Ray Walburg. We did a front and back course approach at Duluth and got a half hour of "actual" logged. On the 9th, I flew 34 Yankee down to Maxwell Prop Shop at Crystal Airport. According to an "AD" (Airworthiness Directive) which I had received, I had to have the props overhauled.

As soon as I got there they rolled her in and had the props off in nothing flat! I watched for awhile and then went to Embers for lunch and checked into a near by motel for the night. The next afternoon they had them done and back on the airplane! I paid them and taxied away being careful to not blow sand into their hangar and get my ass chewed again.

On October 18th, I flew another 1.2 hours with Ray Walburg for my six month multi check ride. I had decided to do that even though it wasn't required. On October 20th, I flew Rory Calhoun, who was a western movie star back in the 50's and 60's down to Stevens Point for a promotion at our Sales and Service Center there! He seemed like a really nice person! On the 29th I flew another 1.1 hours with Ray Walburg for a multi-instrument check ride. I only flew about thirty-two hours in October!

In November I flew another 35 hours all around Minnesota and Wisconsin and North Dakota. I took Joe out to Grand Forks, North Dakota on the 10th and came back the 11th! Northland bought a Sales Center in Rice Lake, Wisconsin so we were landing there often now too!

I got to meet Carl, the weather man and airport manager. Carl would always give me a weather briefing before I'd leave there. I was still a young and in-experienced pilot so I always appreciated and respected what Carl had to say. Once I canceled out going back to Duluth one evening because of Carl's forecast. He was right too!

December 1969 was a busy month! We started the month off by flying down to Sioux Falls, South Dakota. We spent a few hours there and then headed down to Sioux City, Iowa. We spent the night there. It was steaks and drinks as usual! (Just one for me though!) And as usual I'd call the wife and talk to the kids and be in bed by nine! The next day it was back to Sioux Falls for a couple of hours and back to Duluth!

On the 4th I flew Dave and Les Mayer, down to Stevens Point, back over to Eau Claire for an hour or so and into Mankato for the night. Dave and Les were making the rounds and delivering the bonus checks to about half of the sales managers before Christmas!

The next day we flew back up to St. Paul and later on over to Ironwood, Michigan to spend the night. As usual it was steaks and drinks. (Just one for me though!) And I'd call home and be in bed by nine! The next day we just hopped back over to Duluth!

The next day I took off with Bud and Joe aboard to visit the other half of the sales centers! Every night it was steaks and drinks again. (Just one for me though!) and I'd call home and be in bed by nine! At every Sales Center we'd stop at, Bud would have all of the employees in for a meeting. Several times he started off the meetings with, "Well, we had a nice flight down here, yesterday. We were at so and so, and so and so, etc., and Les had his usual exciting time last night. He had supper and was in bed by nine."

Of course, what they didn't know was that in order for me to make a seven-thirty or eight o'clock takeoff, I was up at 5:30 in the morning! Plus if I had flown "instruments" all day and in and out of several sales centers, I was beat! Even though the autopilot in 34 Yankee worked good, I always figured I'd become a better pilot if I flew it, not some black box in the back of the airplane!

That might have been the very flight out of Duluth that the weather was about a 50 feet ceiling with one-quarter mile visibility! I was taking off on runway "09" and the tower was up in the fog so they had asked me to call the tower when I was airborne! The weather was IFR all over Minnesota and Wisconsin.

I had 120 gallons of fuel on board plus three people and baggage. So we were kind of heavy! I don't know why, looking back on it today, that I decided to use some flaps, with 10,000 feet of runway, but I had. We took off and within fifty feet, I was in the fog. I reported airborne – as requested – to the tower. After about 200 feet, I reached over and flipped the flaps up. That got exciting! 34 Yankee rolled forty-five degrees to the left before I could reach over and put the flaps back down and got her flying wings level again!

Somehow it dawned on me, in that instant that the flaps are spring-loaded up and the right one must have frozen in the down position and didn't come up with the left one! The tops of the clouds were about three thousand feet, so I reached down and "spooled" up the turbo's and we hustled up on top, out into the sun! The temperature had been about twenty degrees on the ground and now up on top it was in the thirties. I left the flaps down for about three minutes and then milked them down a little, to break the ice – if in fact that was the problem – and then milked them up. They both came up so – problem solved and away we went!

Since we were in the ice fog, my passengers couldn't see the horizon or anything so they weren't even aware what had happened! I said, "Thank you God" though.

Come to think about it, just a couple flights before, I was at the T-hangar by 6:30 in the morning, getting 34 Yankee ready to make an 8:00 A.M. takeoff. I had a little '67 blue Mustang then. I also had a telescoping tow bar and had put an eye bolt in the front bumper to attach the tow bar to. I also had a twelve volt plug, hanging out of the grill to plug the heater into. I had a twenty pound bottle LP gas heater that I had fired up and I had run a duct to each engine. It was about zero degrees and I wanted to pre-heat 34 Yankee for about an hour.

I got back in the car and moved it ahead until the toe bar locked in. Then I sat and read the morning paper and drank a couple cups of coffee until about 7:30. I got out and opened the cabin door on the airplane and, made sure the mixtures where in idle cutoff, the throttles were closed and the mags (magnetos) were off. I shut down the heater, removed the heat duct from the right engine and pulled the prop through a few times to loosen up the engine. Then I removed the heat duct from the left engine, put the heater back where I kept it, and pulled the left prop through.

The next thing I know is that I'm standing in front of a running engine! I had the presence of mind to not make any quick moves because the hangar floor had ice and snow on it. I didn't know why that engine was running but I figured, it can't run long and it ain't going anyplace because it's hooked to the car. About three seconds later it stopped running.

I thought, "What the hell caused that! I went back and opened the cabin door and confirmed the mixtures were closed, the throttles were closed, and then I looked down under the left control column, so I could see the mag switches. They were all down, in the off position, except for the far switch, it was up. I had a "hot" left mag on the left engine! Once again I said, "Thank you God!"

Even though I had done a lot of things right – I had it hooked to the car so it wasn't going to move ahead, the throttles and mixtures were closed, I had propped it correctly. But the "hot mag" could have cost me a hand, arm, or maybe my life!

I had always heard that if you pulled a prop through backwards, the vacuum pump could fail. Well, that was the last time I've pulled an engine through the way it runs! I've pulled a lot of them backwards and have never, to my knowledge, lost a vacuum pump because of it! In fact I've only lost four or five vacuum pumps in the forty-two years and 10-13,000 hours I've been flying! I was almost "not smart enough" too late!

After that incident, I pulled 34 Yankee out of the hangar, left the tow bar on it and connected to the car, started it up and ran the heater, while I making sure she was ready to go! By the time my passengers got there, I had the chill out of the cabin and all was ready to go.

And, I had worked an hour and a half already and come close to losing a hand or getting killed! I wasn't going to tell them about what happened either. And I don't think I ever did. I thought, ("Hmmm, I don't want them to know that I am the dumbest kid in the world"!)

On December 29, 1969, I started working on getting an Instructor rating at Duluth Airways, with Carl Lucas. We flew again on January 8th and 9th and I left on the 10th with Dave, Bud, and Ray Porter, for Louisville, Kentucky with a fuel stop in Rockford, Illinois. It was the Mobile Home

Manufacturers annual trade show. They spared no expense! Every manufacturer had a hospitality room complete with drinks and snacks. On top of that, they put on a humongous evening buffet! Because of all the visits I had made to the factories with, Dave, Bud, Joe and others and since I was the Director of Customer Relations they had a name tag for me too and I got to attend!

Because I wasn't flying the next day, I could have three drinks! We were up on top floor of the hotel in a circular bar room with windows all around looking out over the city of Louisville on a beautiful clear night. I was standing talking to a couple of guys and I noticed a salesman from one of the sales centers talking to a couple of ladies across the room. The ladies were really pretty; they were wearing lots of makeup, short skirts, low-cut blouses. They might have been chewing gum even! They left and--------- came over and talked to us. I asked him where did those pretty ladies go that you were talking to. He said, "I gave them each fifty bucks and my key so they could go down and wake up--------. The next morning, while I was going through the lobby on the way to have breakfast, I noticed ----------and ---------- with their bags at the front desk and checking out!

We stayed in Louisville until the 15th and I filed IFR for Rockford, Ill where we stopped for fuel again. I got "34Yankee" fueled up, we hit the bathroom and departed IFR to Duluth. We were on top at eight thousand feet, "Fox, Delta, Alpha, Hotel!" ("F"at "D"umb "A"nd "H"appy).

But, my learning experiences weren't over yet! About forty miles out, from Duluth, center dropped us down to six (thousand feet). Thirty miles out they handed me off to Duluth approach who then gave me the weather as 500 feet overcast and a mile visibility. I was told to descend to 4,000 feet, and in a few minutes, to make a left turn to 270 degrees, radar vectors for the ILS "0 9" approach at Duluth. I had noticed on the way down that the tops were at 5,000.

We weren't down to 4,000 but for a few minutes, and I had a quarter inch of ice on the wings already! I thought, ("Hmmm, we're going to be another fifteen-twenty minutes by the time we get out beyond the outer marker and turn north a while and then northeast to intercept the localizer. Then we would get to the outer marker and descend to about, 1,900 feet before we get out of the ice! At the rate this ice is building up, a quarter inch in three minutes, divided into twenty minutes, that's going to be about two inches of ice!"

This is one of the few times I've had some serious doubts about the outcome of a flight! But a little concern (read fear) is good sometimes. As long as you don't allow it to build to the point of mentally locking you up, it prompts action!

So, I called Duluth approach control and told them I was "getting a little to much ice to go out beyond "Pikla" the outer marker, for the whole approach. And by now, I figured, I had too much ice to climb back up on top to get out of it too! I had the ADF (Automatic Direction Finder) tuned to the outer marker and we were just south of it, so I asked approach for a right turn direct to "Pikla," the outer marker. He gave it to mc with a descent to 3,300 and cleared me for the approach.

I think he could tell I needed to get out of the ice and soon! I just kept the needle about five degrees to the right of the nose, on the ADF, and when the localizer needle made the first indication that it was going to move, I made a right turn to "090" and started following the localizer and glideslope down. At least, I knew enough by now to keep my speed up and the bank shallow so as not to stall the airplane!

I looked out at the inner wing root leading edge and saw that I had an inch of ice, and I knew I was flying an "experimental" airplane! I decided not to use flaps, and to keep the gear up until the last minute and I was going to fly it right down to the runway and land with "cruise power!" I figured,

"What the hell, I've got 10,000 feet to get it stopped in!"

Dave and the other guys had noticed the ice on the wings and tip tanks and, maybe, a little sweat, on me too, so they weren't saying anything. They knew I was busy enough!

We popped out of the overcast right about 500 feet above the ground, as the weather said, right on the localizer and right on the glideslope! I dropped the gear, and got a green, down and locked, light! My plan was working out good so far and I flew "34 Yankee right down to and on to the runway by just leveling it out, not even a flare! I got her on in the first five hundred feet, closed the throttles, and made the mid-field turn off!

I think we all kissed the ground after that one!

But it must not have scared Dave very much because a couple of days later, on the 19th we flew down to Minneapolis and landed at the Anoka County airport and came right back to Duluth! ("Hmmm, of course it was also a clear blue day.")

I was gone again just about every day except for the 24th when I got another lesson in the 150 with Carl, for the Instructor rating. While I was over there, talking to Carl and Terry, I told them about my hair- raising experience with the ice. Terry said, "Why didn't you just tell approach you wanted to stay on top until you intercepted the glideslope? I said, "Because nobody ever told me you can do that!" Back then I thought you had to do exactly what you were told to do! (Just like with the wife!) I was just about, "not smart enough, too late" again!

The next week I called ----------to talk to -------- and he didn't work there anymore! I guess---------didn't like being woke up like that!

In, February 1970, I flew eleven trips-three of them overnighters. On the 25th I took Joe Sebastien to Grand Forks, Fargo, and Minot and spent the night. Same thing--

steaks and drinks, (just one for me though!) call home, and in bed by nine!

The next morning it was 300-400 feet overcast with a mile visibility. Joe had brought his tape recorder with him and wanted to tape the whole trip back to Duluth! I thought, ("Hmmm, is this for some kind of evidence in case we crash or what?")

Joe started the tape as I was reading the checklist and starting the engines. He kept taping as I called for a IFR clearance and when I got the clearance and, pretty soon, the release, calling center etc. The best part is, on the climb out you can hear the ice coming off the right prop, hitting the nose of the airplane! Being we were going to be gone for a few days Joe's wife had driven him the airport so she could have the car while he was gone. So I gave Joe a ride home, and then he invited me in and "made" me drink a couple of beers. What could I do, he was bigger than me!! Joe's daughter Barbara asked Joe if she could have $35.00 to take a bus to Prairie Du Chien, Wisconsin to visit her grandpar-

1966 Twin Comanche N8034Y

ents and cousins. I knew she liked to paint, so I told her I'd give her the $35.00 if she'd paint a picture of "34Yankee" for me. I gave her $35.00 and here's the picture she painted. Not bad for a teenager I thought!

I still hear from Joe once in awhile. His first marriage failed. Then he moved to Chattanooga, Tennessee and has been selling insurance since. Joe was from Prairie du Chien, Wisconsin. He calls me once in awhile when he's coming up to visit his family. I've flown my 310 down there and visited with him and his girlfriend, Ellie. I've given rides up and down the Mississippi River in my 310 to Joe and Ellie and some of his other family members.

Joe called me a couple of years ago to tell me that he and Ellie were going to get married on Valentines Day 1998 and they hoped I could make it! I said, "Joe, stop and think this over. Don't let her rush you into anything! Back off a little, you've only been living with her for twenty years! They got married on Valentines Day!

I didn't get another lesson in with Carl until February 28th! In March I flew just about every day again with Northland, with four trips being overnighters! And of course, it was steaks and drinks every night! (Just one for me though!)

I didn't get a chance to fly with Carl at all in March! On April 2nd I did get a lesson in. I got one again on the 7th,and another on the 8th and then not again until the 16th and 17th! The rest of the month I was gone with "Northland again! I loved it though!

Except, one day I was walking in downtown Duluth, and I looked in a store window and thought, "Who's that fat kid?" It was me! The steaks and drinks and sitting in an airplane or office was catching up to me! When I started flying for Northland, I was probably 150 pounds, because I had just finished building the mobile home park. Now I was 185! Of course, the burnt-orange leisure suit I had on probably didn't help either! When I was home, it was potatoes and gravy, ice cream and cookies, etc.

It was then and there that I decided to start changing my eating habits and get more exercise.

Whenever the weather was bad enough that I wanted to cancel the trip, I'd call Dave, Bud, Joe or whoever was flying with me that day and ask, "Have you got anything so important to do today that it's worth dying for?" I never had anyone ever try to pressure me into going, when I called to cancel or delay the takeoff! (Of course I had probably scared the shit out of them so many times already that they knew, if I didn't want to go, it must be, really, really, really bad up there!)

On May 4th I got another lesson in with Carl doing ground reference maneuvers, chandelles, cross-wind takeoffs and landings, etc. for about an hour and a half. Then I was gone again for a couple of days, got another lesson on the seventh and that was it for the month of May 1970!

Every month I had to find a free day and get "34 Yankee" into maintenance, to change the oil, and un-cowl her to see if anything was about to fall off!

About the only problems I ever had with "34 Yankee" was with the turbo waste gates. Every once in awhile Jerry Bergman, the mechanic, would have to do some welding on them. The few days I was in the office I was busy doing my "customer relations" job! One thing nice about flying for Northland, besides all the great people and steaks and drinks, I was almost always home on weekends!

This was about the time that I'd meet another person that would become important to me. And, become a life long friend! His name is Ed Sutton. Ed was hired as a District Manager. He was also a pilot and had owned a 170 but hadn't flown much recently. Once in awhile he liked to fly "34 Yankee", from the right seat, if he wasn't busy doing paper work. Ed is the kind of person you like from the start--big smile, talkative, always up-beat, and friendly!

Ed's first marriage had failed a couple of years before I met him. But, he told me that he was helping out at a church supper and the cook said, "Ed, drive over to Superior, to the college, and there will be a girl standing on the corner of "such, and such." She needs a ride over here so she can help too!" So Ed drives over to Superior, finds the corner of "such and such", picks up the girl and gives her a ride back to the church. It turns out she was, "First runner-up for Miss Oklahoma in 1961" and her name was Roberta Reed.

Well, Ed is also a very good looking, athletic type guy so it was almost mutual instant love I suspect! They had just gotten married January 16th of 1970. It wasn't long and I got to meet Roberta. She was not only very pretty, but, very smart and very kind too! She was also a teacher.

When, I first met them they were living in a little log cabin up the north shore a ways. After a few months they moved into Duluth between where I lived and the airport. If Ed was flying with me that day I'd stop and pick him up on the way to the airport--unless it was in the winter when I had to be at the hangar an hour and half earlier! When I'd stop to pick up Ed, Roberta would give him a hug and kiss and tell him she'd miss him. And then she'd give me a hug, (no kiss though – she must have liked Ed better than me!) and she'd say, "Les, you take good care of Ed now and you guys have a fun and safe trip!"

When we'd get home Roberta, or "Bertie" for short, would run out to the car if she saw us drive up and give Ed a hug and kiss and tell him she missed him. Then she'd give me hug and thank me for getting Ed home safely. She was just like Ed, always pleasant and up-beat.

When I'd get home, I was always excited if the wife's car was in the garage, but then I'd be disappointed because I never got a "welcome home", like most of my friends did. (I hadn't realized what I was missing until I saw how good some of my friends had it!) I had always been a little envious of the way Peggy doted over Johnson all the time. If he just went out to feed the cattle and horses for a half an hour, he'd get a hug and kiss when he came back in! At first I was envious of Johnson; now I'm envious of Ed too!

My wife was a good woman, she was a hard worker, kept the house well, was a good cook, took good care of the kids, but wasn't very demonstrative. And when I think back, neither were her parents. And I suppose neither were my parents. Once in awhile I'd see my dad grab my mother and kind of waltz her around a little in the kitchen. (He must have done a lot more than that at least ten times in the bedroom though!)

I got another lesson in with Carl on the 2nd and 3rd of June and on the 6th again, with a trip with Northland to Minneapolis, Marshfield and back to Duluth on the 4th . Then I flew steady with Northland through the 18th!! I got lessons with Carl on the 19th 20th, 22nd, 24th, and 26th ! We flew again on July 6th and 7th.

On the 9th my mechanic and friend Jerry Bergman, let me fly his beautiful J3 on floats for a couple of hours. I took it over to Cloquet and landed on Big Lake, about ten miles west of Cloquet, and visited Byron and Lloyd at their cabins.

I flew with Carl again on the 10th and on the 11th, Carl signed me off to go take the checkride! On the 13th I flew down to Minneapolis' Wold Chamberlain Airport and checked in at the GADO (General Aviation District Office) office.

I introduced my self to the lady at the desk and she said, "You will be flying with Mr. Watson." I almost said, "You know what, I think I'm having an appendix attack! Re-schedule me with someone else, maybe tomorrow."

It was common knowledge around the coffee machine that if you got Mr. Watson, you weren't going to pass the first time! But then I figured, "I'm here, might as well give it my best shot!"

Soon, Mr. Watson came over and introduced himself. We chatted a little. He wanted to know what I did for a living etc. He looked over my log book and paperwork. I had 1,301.1hrs TT (Total Time) 608hrs SE (Single Engine) 666hrs Multi (two engines) and 17.3hrs on floats. (seaplane), 152hrs night time and 125hrs actual instrument time. I was high time I thought!

He said, "Go into one of those rooms over there and draw four ground reference maneuvers on the blackboard and I'll be back in ten minutes." Ten minutes later he came in, sat down, pulled his telescoping pointer out of his inside suit pocket, and said, "Teach me how to do those."

Things were going along pretty good until I got to a maneuver called "turns on a point". He asked, "Where will the steepest bank occur doing turns on a point?" I had, at least I thought I had, been taught that the greater the ground speed, the steeper the bank. I had shown the wind as out of the north at 10kts. So, I said, "Right here, when I'm heading south." I was turning left. "Are you sure about that?" he asked? I said, "Yes sir". (I can be really polite when I know I'm in trouble!)

I must have done OK, on the others, because he got away from the turns on a point and started asking questions about FAR's part 61, 91 and 135. (Federal Aviation Regulations) At least this is where "I shined!" I knew 61's and 91's verbatim and enough 135 to get by back then!

He asked me a few questions, then smiled and said, "Let's go fly." We took off and headed southwest until we were out of town. The first thing he wanted was a turn on a point. I don't know how I could have been so stupid! Obviously, there it was – directly cross wind on the up-wind side!

Then he asked me to do a full power, full flap stall. I had never done one before. So I did a full power, full flap stall, and wiggled off about ten degrees both sides of the "270"degrees, that I was supposed to be heading.

He said, "Man, haven't you never done these before?" I said, "No sir." "Let me show you," he said. He did one and the DG stayed glued on "270"degrees!" I did another and stayed within five degrees so he got off that.

Then he said, "Give me a slip to the left with the nose on horizon and note the airspeed let's say it was fifty, give me a slip to the right with the nose on the horizon and note the airspeed, let's say it was sixty. He said, "Man, how come the airspeed is so much slower when we slip to the left than when we slip to the right?" "Dammed if I know," I'm thinking. Mr. Watson knew I didn't know too!

But all of a sudden it dawned on me! I said, "I know why, because of the static port being on the left side of the airplane! When we slip to the left, we're pressurizing it; when we slip to the right, we're creating a low pressure area on that side of the airplane!

We did a few other things and headed back to Wold Chamberlain. They were using runways, "29 Left" and "29 Right". (It was 29 back then; it's 30 now.) We got "29 Left." He said, "Let's do a short field landing. I said, "Mr. Watson, I heard a Northwest heavy clear the marker a minute ago. How about a cross-wind landing so we can get on and off before that Northwest gets here. That was fine with him and besides there was a pretty good cross wind anyway! I lucked out and "kissed it" on the upwind gear followed by the downwind and the nose gear and taxied in.

When we got back up to the office, Mr. Watson went over and talked to Andy Detroi for a few minutes and then came back over to me and said, "Mr. Hubbell, I'm going to give you an instructor rating." And he filled out the paper work. I thanked him and I headed back to Duluth. I was north of the Grantsburg VOR about ten miles when it really hit me that I had passed the first time! I pushed the nose of that 150 down and pulled up sharply and did a wing over and said, "Whoopie, I passed! Who says 13 is an unlucky number! It was July 13, 1970. (And I thought, ("Hmmm, maybe I'm only about the 550th dumbest kid in the world!")

The next morning at the coffee machine I informed Carl, Terry, Jim and anybody else in earshot that I had found Mr. Watson to be one of the nicest and fairest examiners I had ever taken a checkride with.

I was gone again with Northland Homes pretty much everyday from the 14th, through the 24th. On the 25th I took Jerry's J3 on floats and flew down to Moose Lake and landed and taxied up to my cousin's dock. I gave Vi and Pat Rizzie's kids a ride in the J3, visited for awhile and headed back to Pike Lake where Jerry lived.

The only irritating' problem I was having with "34 Yankee" was that once in awhile I couldn't transmit on my Number One Com radio! The radio shop had pulled that radio at least three times and sent it to the factory once! It would work for maybe a week or maybe a day.

I was having coffee with Terry and Carl one morning and mentioned the radio problem and Terry said, "Have you ever tried that guy down at Superior? I said, "I didn't know there was anybody down there." He said that his name is Ray Maybrey and he looked up his telephone number for me.

So I called him, introduced myself, and told him about all the radio problems I'd been having and what had been done. He said, "Hell that problem ain't even in the radio!" I asked, "Where is it then?" He said, "It's the transmitter relay sole-noid in the back of the airplane!" I said, "Have you got one on hand?" He said, "Sure". I said, "If I fly down there have you got time to replace it?" He said, "It will only take me five minutes; come on down. So I pulled "34 Yankee" out of the hangar and flew down to the Superior airport.

Ray's office was a pilot house off of some old ore boat! I taxied up and shut down and before I was out of the airplane he had the baggage door open and the back bulkhead off. In another two minutes he closed it up and asked, "Was it working on the way down here?" I said, "No." He said, "I'll go inside and you call me on unicom, 122.8." I made two or three transmissions and it worked every time that day and every time thereafter too! Ray Maybrey was my avionics guy after that!

After he set up shop down at Anoka Airport I'd get in there every once in awhile. One time he was taking his T28 up to check it out and asked me if I wanted to go with. Of course I did! Another time he had his "DC3" down to Austin, Minnesota. (They were having a pancake breakfast there.) I caught a ride back to Anoka in it with him and some other guys.

One day I had my "310" in his shop getting the pitot static re-certifications done and he was going to take his "T33" up to check something out. "Want to go with me Les?" I was almost in the back seat before he got to the airplane! He just took off, climbed out staying in the pattern, and made a long downwind and came back in and landed.

It was maybe, a year later when I was watching the news one evening and they announced a local pilot had crashed at Selfridge Air National Guard Base over in Detroit. I had heard during the day that it was Ray. As I watched, I saw the "T33" roll. When the tip tank hit the ground, it just exploded.

I had never seen a friend of mine die in an airplane before, it was especially traumatic for me in that I had flown in the "T33" with Ray before. It was very, very hard to watch knowing the fear he must have been feeling at that moment. It brought memories of my brother Van back to me. The thought occurred to me, "If it can happen to Ray, it can happen to me too."

I flew just about every day right up until September 19th and then didn't fly for two weeks! I almost felt like I'd have to be re-trained again! On October 5th we started flying all around the upper mid-west again! On the 8th we went to Minot and Devils Lake and spent the night at Grand Forks, North Dakota. Yup, it was steaks and drinks again! (Just one for me though!) Then I called home, talked to the wife and kids and was in bed by nine!

The next day we departed Grand Forks for Fargo, spent a hour or so there, went to Alexandria, spent a hour or so there, went to Flying Cloud, spent an hour there, went to Eau Claire, spent a couple of hours there, had steaks and drinks--none for me though – and then flew back to Duluth! That was a long day and I was a tired puppy when we landed at Duluth! I still thought though, "There isn't much of anything prettier than a full IFR runway all lit up at night!"

On Sunday morning, October 12th one of Jeno's (Paulucci) pilots, Ralph Hughes, called me to see if I'd ride right seat for him in the Falcon because Jeno had decided to go to St. Paul and none of their other pilots were home.

That was the first time I ever had a chance to fly in a jet so of course I went with him! Jeno was staying in St. Paul a few days so Ralph and I just taxied out, took off and flew back to Duluth. That Falcon would probably be landing in St. Paul before I'd cross the St. Louis River, south of Duluth, with the Twin Comanche if we had taken off together! But-- that's the difference between the men and boys, the price of their toys.

On October 17th we loaded up the whole family, including Ginger our golden lab, into "34 Yankee" and flew out to Johnsons to visit and hunt pheasants. I made the standard low pass over Johnson's house and then went down and landed at DeSmet. Soon Johnson, Peggy and their girls arrived to pick us up. It's a good thing they had a Suburban because we filled it up, with Ginger across two laps!

The kids had fun visiting with the Johnson girls, Elizabeth, Laura and now Melinda Jane! As always, we had a great visit and the hunting was good! We flew back to Duluth late afternoon the next day with a limit of pheasants and full stomachs.

Before 1970 ended I had put another sixty hours on 34 Yankee with Northland! And I was having fun doing it!

Flying in 1971 started out on January 5th with me flying Dave over to Green Bay, down to Manitowoc, and back to Green Bay. We stayed two days and got back to Duluth late on the seventh. Of course, it was still steaks and drinks, call home, and in bed by nine! I was always excited to get home. The kids were always glad to see me, but the wife hardly acknowledged that I was home. I had heard lots of "I love you", but I was sensing, something wasn't right in my marriage.

On the 12th it was back over to Green Bay with Bud for a couple of hours and back to Duluth. On the fourteenth I flew Dave and Bud down to Louisville, Kentucky for the annual "Mobile Homes Manufacturers show. Once again there was no end to the hospitality rooms full of food and drinks! And of course as Director of Customer Relations for Northland Homes, I was a guest also! I liked my job with Northland Homes! Everybody was super great to me!

After we got back, we didn't go anyplace for a week, which gave me time to get my office work done and to catch up on my "home life!" But on the 22nd we left and were gone again, almost everyday for the rest of January!

We didn't fly at all the first week of February! On the 8th I took Dave down to Minneapolis and back and then we didn't fly again until the 17th! After that though we flew just about every day! Some place in between flights I had to get "34 Yankee" in for oil changes and, an annual inspection!

During the first half of March I was gone again through the 13th and then home for a week. On the 17th I flew Joe Sebastien to Fargo, Grand Forks, Fargo and back to Duluth. I still remember when we were in "position and hold on

35L" at Grand Forks, waiting for a release. The wind was blowing so strong right down the runway that my airspeed was showing 60 miles per hour! And the snow was blowing so much I could hardly see fifty feet down the runway! But I could look up and see blue sky! We got released and I was airborne before we'd rolled a hundred feet and before I even got the throttles three quarters to the wall! I think it only took about fifteen minutes to get to Fargo that day!

Sometime in the first part of April, Dave called me into his office and told me the shareholders were pressuring him to cut expenses, and he was going to have to cut "34 Yankee" out of the budget. I could tell he felt as bad as I did that he had to tell me that.

I said, "How are you going to get around to all the sales centers?" He said, "I don't know; I sure don't want to go back to driving." He wanted me to stay on as the Director of Customer Relations but I had gotten the "flying bug" too bad to just quit flying and I told him that. He understood and was, super considerate of me. He said, "Well, just do it until you get another flying job, if that will help you." I liked flying for Northland Homes and I knew I was going to miss all the nice people! I made my last flight for Northland on May 18, 1971. I had three drinks that night.

Chapter Seventeen

Halvair Years
1971-1977

Soon after the word was out that I wasn't flying for Northland Homes anymore, I got a call from Fred Winship, the chief pilot for Halvair. Halvair was a new FBO at Duluth. The Halvorson family had built it about a year earlier. Fred wanted to know if I'd fly for them.

I went over and we discussed it. I asked him how much he'd pay me. He said, "We'll pay you what you're worth." I said, "I can't live on that!" A week later we reached an agreement and I started on May 31, 1971 by flying a 310 up to Grand Rapids to take a single engine proficiency check ride with Gordy Newstrom.

The Halvorsons had also bought Mesaba Aviation at Grand Rapids from Gordy, and Gordy had become the check pilot for both operations then. Fred needed to get the 310 to Grand Rapids and a 172 back to Duluth, so this would "kill two birds with one stone." I said, "Fred, I've never flown a 310 before." He said, "It's just a fat Twin Comanche." I said, "OK, as long as you know that!"

So I flew the 310 up there, took a check ride with Gordy in a 172 and flew it back to Duluth! On June 2nd I took a standardization hop in a Cessna 150. That's how Fred wrote it up in my logbook. Later that same day Fred gave me an official checkout in the 310 while we made a trip to St. Paul and back.

The next day, June 3rd I flew with my first three students: Roland Hanson, Earl King and Jon Klasen. The next day I made a charter trip in a 172 to Rhinelander in central Wisconsin and back! On the 6th I flew a Cessna 402 up to Grand Rapids and brought a 421 back to Duluth, with Carl as my co-pilot and instructor again. Carl, Terry and Jim were working for Halvair now.

Terry Anderson had become Halvorson's pilot. They were flying a "690" Commander at that time and moved up to a Saberliner a couple of years later.

On June 7th Fred brought me another student-Steve Rablers, and on June 8th Earl King and Bruce Wakefield. On June 11th he brought Don Hudson, and I flew with him for an hour. I signed up Tom Buchanan on June 12th and flew with him for 1.2 hours. On the 13th and 16th I checked Lloyd Grindahl out in a Cherokee 140 he had bought.

On the 14th I signed up Jack Jones and flew with him for half an hour to see if he was going to like flying or not. Jack was a professor over at the college and had wanted to learn to fly for years. After lunch I got a checkout in the 210 N9471 Mike and an hour later I flew two guys down to Kansas City and Wichita, Kansas in it.

We spent the night in Wichita, but there weren't any steaks and drinks anymore! I ate in a little diner, called the wife and kids, and was still in bed by nine though! The next day we flew back to Minneapolis. We spent a couple of hours there and then went back to Duluth!

On the 16th, I took Ed Sutton and his dad Ken over to Tomahawk, Wisconsin so Ken could look at a welder he was thinking of buying. Here it was, only two weeks later, after I left Northland, and between students and chartering, I had a full time job again!

Everyday I'd fly with three or four students! I soloed my first student, Tom Buchanan, the morning of June 17th, 1971. The next day I soloed Steve Rablers with 7.9 hours – eleven days after he started!

Early afternoon on June 20th I took "34 Yankee" up to Grand Rapids and showed her to Dr. Muller. It was a sad day for me, but I knew I wasn't going to be flying her enough to justify keeping her.

In the afternoon I checked Johnny Johnson out in the 172 for .9 of an hour. Johnny had a transmission shop and raced cars up at the Proctor Speedway.

On the morning of June 21st I flew with Jack Jones for an hour, with Tom Buchanan for thirty minutes, soloed Gary Lillness, took George and Jan--who were from Alaska--on a scenic flight down over the Duluth harbor. After lunch I flew with Bill Radtke for an hour. We took a break and talked and then flew for another hour and de-briefed for thirty minutes.

Then I had the sad experience of delivering 34 Yankee to Dr. Muller. The wife must have known it was going to be a very emotional thing for me to do and volunteered to go with me. We flew up and met with Dr. Muller at the Grand Rapids Airport. He gave me a check and I gave him a bill of sale and registration, and he flew us back to Duluth. When we got to Duluth, I told him to just shut down the right engine and we'll bail out. I had tears in my eyes when he started it up and taxied away; even the wife was crying! (I don't think she'd cry if I was leaving!)

On June 23rd I soloed Bill Radtke and signed up Don Hudson! On the 25th I delivered a Cessna 182 to Des Moines, for the aircraft sales manager, Gene Berg, and caught a jet back to Duluth.

On the 28th I had my first charter in the 310! I flew three people down to Chicago Meigs Airport and back. It was fun going to Meigs. One minute I'm in Duluth; two and a half hours later I'm on the edge of Lake Michigan looking at the Chicago skyline! It was a beautiful June day! I thought, ("Hmmm, I'm glad I wasn't really too dumb to be a pilot!)

July started out busy. I was flying with three or four students every day! Jack Jones and I were flying one of the 150s on the 5th --N6828G. We had been doing "take off's and landings" on Runway "27". By now I had determined it was a waste of time to make just one takeoff and landing on a 10,000ft runway so I got approval from the tower to do multiple takeoffs and landings – thus saving the student a lot of time and money!

Jack and I had been in a left-hand pattern for about thirty minutes when the tower asked us to make a right hand pattern because of some traffic they had approaching from the northwest. I figured that it was good practice for Jack to do something different and everything was going smoothly until we were on a right base leg..

I called the tower and said, "Can you confirm that "28 Golf" is cleared to land?" The tower replied, "Roger 28 Golf, you're cleared to land." I said, "Does that "101" in the left overhead know that?" The tower then said, "28 Golf make an immediate left 360!" He didn't really have to tell me; I was already doing it!!" I thought, ("Hmmm, a person could get killed up here!")

On the 6th I flew the "310", N5733 Mike over to Madeline Island and picked up three people and flew them to Minneapolis, Mankato, Marquette, Escanaba, Green Bay, and back to Madeline Island, dropped them off, and flew back to Duluth. It was a long day but I enjoyed it! And I was finding myself really getting to like the 310!

For the next week, I flew with my students, Earl King, Bill Radtke, Ross Peterson, Jack Jones and Tom Buchanan. I was enjoying instructing! On the 13th I got my first multi student, Chris Tervo. Chris was going to go to Alaska and fly. On July 21 Don Hudson soloed!

On July 22nd I had a charter flight in the "210" N9471 Mike from Duluth to Hibbing. I picked up two guys and flew them down to Wold Chamberlain to catch an airline flight and flew alone back to Duluth.

On July 23rd I flew with my friend Ed Sutton and checked him out in the 172 N84882. I had charter flights in the 210 again on July 24, 25, and 26!

When I got back on July 26th the chief pilot, Fred Winship, introduced me to Mike Gardonio. Mike had been a helicopter pilot in Vietnam. Mike was to be my first commercial student. We flew 1.4 hours that day and usually an hour and a half every couple of days after that. On July 27th I got another private student, Jean Sundholm.

August was just like July! Students and charters every day! On August 5th I signed up and flew with Vic Thompson. "Vic" owned the Standard station down on the freeway. I soloed Jean on the 9th. On the 13th I went to Winnipeg and back with the 310. On the 15th I had another 310 charter to Chicago Midway and back.

On August 24th I flew Miss Minnesota to Valley City, North Dakota for a beauty pageant! Were there ever a lot of beautiful women in Valley City that day! On August 26th I checked Ed Sutton out in the 182!

September of 1971 was another busy month! I was enjoying it though! It was gratifying to watch my students learning to fly.

Chris Tervo was my first student for the day on September 2nd When he arrived he said, "Hi Les." I said, "It ain't Les to you anymore – It's Mr. Hubbell. In fact, worse yet, it's Examiner Hubbell to you. From now on I don't give a damn about you! I don't care how much money you've got, what kind of car you drive, and I don't care about your wife and kids. All I want to know is if you know the regulations, the aircraft manual, and can you fly the airplane! Sit down this is your oral! I did a complete "Jeckel and Hyde," asking him one question after the other and once in awhile I said, "How come you don't know that? I know your instructor covered that with you, etc., etc."

Nobody passed the first time – maybe the second or third!

The next day Chris and I went through another "Jekyll and Hyde" session and I recommended him for his multi-check ride! He took it with Gordy Newstrom a few days later and passed! When he came back he told me Gordy hadn't been nearly as demanding as I had! I said, "Yes, but did he give a damn about how much money you have or what kind of car you drive or your wife and kids or did he just want to know if you knew the regulations, the manual, and if you could fly the airplane? He said, "No, he didn't care nothing about me and yes he only wanted to know if I knew the regulations, manual and if I could fly the airplane, I guess." I said, "Well, that's why I played the part, so you'd know what to expect the examiner to be like." (Besides, it was fun!)

On September 7th, Mike Gardonio was my first victim, I mean, my first student of the day. He found me heading for the coffee machine and said, "Can I buy you a cup of coffee Les? I said, "No you can't! In fact, it ain't Les to you anymore. It's Mr. Hubbell. In fact, worse yet, it's examiner Hubbell! Get your coffee and meet me down in my office and bring the aircraft manual!"

I went into my "Jeckel and Hyde" routine and we spent an hour and a half on the oral and then went out and flew the airplane. Mike had been a helicopter pilot in VietNam and I was always impressed how well he could hold heading and altitude. He was doing very well. I'd usually only have to show him something once and after that it was like clockwork.

On the 9th I flew under the hood in the 172 with Terry Anderson. We spent 1.7 hours, flying up to Grand Rapids, did the VOR approach, a lot of basic instrument flying, unusual attitudes, steep turns, slow flight etc., and then the ILS 09 into Duluth.

On the 13th I flew with Carl doing a basic instrument review and he signed me off for the "instrument instructor check flight. On the 15th I flew up to International Falls and took the checkride with Bob Winterude from the Minneapolis GADO. (General Aviation District Office) The oral was all about the compass and only lasted about ten minutes and then we went out and of course he flew the airplane.

I started him out with a ITO off Runway "31". Then we spent an hour and a half doing all of the approaches and landed. Bob filled out my paper work and I commented, "That was the easiest checkride I've ever taken." He said, "Well, you've got an instructor rating and an instrument rating; I just wanted to find out if you could talk!" I thanked him and flew back to Duluth!

In September I also started doing a lot of flying in the "210" with Reserve Mining. Just about every day or two we'd fly for four to five hours going all the way up the North shore of Lake Superior, checking to see where the green-looking water was coming from. Reserve Mining and my students kept me very busy in September!

The morning of the September 21st I went through the Jeckel and Hyde routine with Roland Hanson and later in the afternoon with Mike Gardonio again and then recommended Mike for his commercial checkride. The morning of September 24th I gave Roland Hanson the Jekel and Hyde treatment again and recommended him for his private checkride. On September 28th I flew the 172 N84882 down to St. Paul for the Instrument Instructor Seminar and flew back to Duluth on October 3rd.

On the morning of October 7th I made my first charter flight from Duluth to Grand Rapids and back for the Goldfine Company of Duluth in the 310 N5733M. After lunch I started Mike Gardonio on the Instrument Rating course. On the 8th and again on the 10th, I flew three guys from the Hallett Company up to International Falls and back in the 310.

On the morning of the 11th Terry Anderson, Jim Nelson and I were at the coffee machine when Mike Gardonio came for his lesson. He got a cup of coffee and started complaining about his new bride's cooking. Jim asked him why he had married her if she can't cook? Mike said, " Because she's good in bed." Jim said, "You dumb s---, they're all good in bed, marry one that can cook!" (I've always wished that had been my line!)

The afternoon of the 11th I started Roland Hanson on his float rating. We flew the Champ on floats for 2.1 hours.

On October 12th I flew Nick Smith to Fargo in the 310, stayed overnight and returned to Duluth the next morning. Nick was one of the shareholders in Northland Homes so he had flown with me several times in "34 Yankee" Nick wasn't comfortable flying in light airplanes and always had a death grip on the assist strap. I called him "white knucks Nick."

I remember one night we were coming back from visiting a few of the sales centers in Stevens Point, Marshfield, Eau Claire, and Rice Lake. It was in March and snowing like crazy, big flakes too! The windshield was glowing with "St. Elmo's fire." I told Nick, "Watch this," and I held my right hand, with my fingers spread, about two inches from the windshield. The "St. Elmo's fire" was dancing from my finger tips to the windshield, which I thought was great fun! Nick grabbed my arm away and said, "Cut that out, I need you alive, to get me back to Duluth!"

The morning of October 13th I flew with Dave Hedin for .7 hours in the 150 and then flew a charter to Fargo and back in the 310. The next morning Roland and I drove out to Pike Lake and flew the Champ on floats, N1511E, for 1.8 hours. After lunch, I flew with Pat Kolquist in a 150. On the morning of the 15th I flew Nick Smith back up to Fargo for a couple of hours and then to Minneapolis for an hour and back to Duluth by early afternoon! Then Roland and I went float flying again for 1.1 hours!

During the next week I flew with my students. On October 22nd I flew a charter in the 310 N 3285X to Glasgow, Montana. We stayed overnight and returned the next day for 7.1 hours of 310 time! I flew with Mike Gardonio on the 25th. We flew for an hour and a half of actual instruments from Duluth to Hibbing, shot the ILS and back to Duluth for the ILS 09. The next day, I recommended Roland for the seaplane checkride.

On October 27th Fred Winship and I flew a charter in the 310, N3285 X-ray. We went up to Hibbing and picked up four people and took them to St. Paul. The whole flight was solid instruments. We barely spotted the runway at St. Paul but made it in. I signed Fred off for 1.3 hours of dual. I flew left seat on the way back and we were again on solid instruments.

About halfway between the Grantsburg VOR and Duluth we got into some turbulence that was tossing the 310 up and down 500 feet! I felt that if I had tried to hold altitude within 300 feet I'd pull the wings off it. So I called center and reported the turbulence and asked for a 1,000ft block of altitude to bounce up and down in, and got it.

After that I just did the best I could to hold a level attitude and let her float up and down so as not to over-stress the airframe. It was so bad that about thirty miles southwest of Duluth I called center and changed our destination from Hibbing to Duluth and called Halvair on the unicom and had them have a van ready to drive the people up to Hibbing.

I told the passengers what I was doing and they were all in favor or it! I was on the back course "27" approach and had it glued, but about a mile from the runway approach gave me a unexpected 30 degree right turn. We landed and taxied in and got the passengers into the van and on their way to Hibbing.

I picked up a phone and called approach and told them I had been right on the centerline and asked them what was the deal with the thirty degree turn? He said he knew I was right on, but there was a strong windshear just ahead in that area and the last two airplanes had gotten blown so far off course that they had to go around for another approach. I said, "OK, but maybe next time tell me ahead of time so I know what we're doing it for."

On October 29th I got to make my first charter in the"421" N8043Q from Duluth to International Falls and return. The next day I took another charter in the "421" to Watertown, South Dakota and back. The next day I flew the "210" up to our sister operation in Grand Rapids and brought a Cardinal back.

On November 3rd I started Kerry Welsh on the private pilot program. In the afternoon I flew with Mike Gardonio for 1.7 hours. I had Mike make a ITO off Runway 27 and then fly the ILS 09 localizer, backwards of course, to the outer marker and into the holding pattern. After a few turns in the holding pattern, we intercepted the localizer, did the ILS 09 down to the decision height.

Mike called a missed approach and I gave him a heading of "090" and told him to climb to 3,100 feet. We went straight out for a back course "27" approach. When we turned inbound approach, control asked me what we wanted to do next after the "27" back-course approach. I told them we wanted to go to the VOR and hold. He came back with a clearance to, "at the missed approach point, turn right to 360 degrees and climb to 3,100 feet and contact approach control", and sent us over to the tower.

Mike called the "missed approach" to the tower, turned right to "360"degrees and started a climbed to 3,100 feet, and tower said to contacted approach control. Approach control gave us a right turn direct to the VOR and told us to hold at 3,100 feet. Mike did a good job getting into the holding pattern and after a couple of turns he had it nailed. I called approach and got a "VOR 31" approach to a full stop and we came in and landed and taxied in.

When we got inside, one of the other instructors said, "Hubbell, call the tower." (I hate it when they say that!) I called the tower and the assistant tower chief asked, "Did that get a little close up there?" I responded, "What do you mean?" He said, "You were supposed to make a left turn to the VOR so we released a DC9 off "09" going to Hibbing and it looked a little close from here." I said, "What the hell are you doing releasing a DC9 off runway "09" with us on final to "27"! "And," I said, "Besides, our missed approach instructions were for a right turn to 360 and up to 3,100 feet. He said, "No they weren't, you were supposed to turn left." I hung up and was really not only embarrassed but stressed because of the mistake. I didn't like making mistakes and still didn't believe I had made this one!

I talked to Mike about it again and he was sure our instructions had been to turn right and climb to 3,100 also. Then I remembered that at the time approach gave us the missed approach instructions, I thought it was kind of strange that he didn't give us a left turn since the VOR was to our left. But then I thought, (Hmmm, he must have some traffic coming from the south) so I didn't give it another thought.

I agonized over what had happened for another half an hour and still couldn't believe I had made such a mistake. In fact, nobody hated making mistakes as much as I did, back then! (now, if I make less that 10 a day I'm happy!)

I called the tower and said I wanted to come over and listen to the tapes. The assistant tower chief said I'd have to wait until morning before he could have them available. I said, "OK, I'll see you in the morning."

I was sure now that I hadn't screwed up so I had lunch and went and flew with Roy Larson for another 1.2 hours and quit a little early.

When I got home the kids and Ginger would always run out to greet me. But when I walked into the house, the wife hardly acknowledged that I was home. I told her what had happened with the tower but got no reaction one way or another. I'm starting to wonder, (Hmmm, maybe the best thing I've ever did in life, was to join the AirForce.)

The next morning about 9:00 I called the tower and Jim Timmons, the tower chief, answered the phone. I told him what had happened and that I wanted to come over and listen to the tapes.

Jim said, "Les, it looks like my people made a mistake so how about we just forget about it?" I said, "Oh sure, when your people screw up, I should just forget about it, but when one of us instructors screws up your assistant tower chief wants to hang our asses out to dry! If I forget this one Jim, how many "free chips" do I get for when one of us does screw up? He said, "You just call me if you have any problems with the assistant tower chief and we'll work it out." I had always liked Jim, he'd come over and talk to us instructors now and then to see if there was anything the tower could do to help us. We had told him a couple of times that the best help he could give us would be to get rid of the assistant tower chief!

The next morning I did an introduction ride with Penny Cook and after that Mike and I did an instrument XC from Duluth to Rochester, to Eau Claire and back to Duluth for five hours worth. The next morning I did the same thing with Rick Alston for another five hours! On November 7, 1971, I started Tom Cook on the private pilot course in the morning and when we got back I did the same thing with his wife, Penny!

A realtor stopped in one evening to tell us how nice our house looked with snow on it etc. and that she had a buyer who was interested in it. I asked her how much she could get us and she came back with a figure that was higher than I expected so I told her we'd think about it. We had been thinking about moving into town so that the kids would have more friends and be closer to school so they could take part in more activities and we wouldn't have to be driving them back and forth for everything.

So after the wife and I discussed it and had a "family vote," we decided to sell and move into town.

I had told myself when I sold Sunnyside though, that I'd never get back into a seven-day-a-week business again. But, I was finding myself working six long days, getting up at 5:30 to make 7:30 takeoffs, and a lot of times not getting back into Duluth until 9:30 that same night, and occasionally working on Sundays too. Besides I had over 2,000 hours total time now!

From November 8th through November 13th I was flying steady with my students with a day off on Sundays usually. On the 15th I had a charter with the Goldfine Company from Duluth to Grand Forks and return.

I liked flying with Monnie and Erv Goldfine. Those guys were like clockwork! If they said we were leaving at 7:30 in the morning, you could have the left engine running and they would be climbing in the door at 7:25! Erv would always sit in the back right seat and have a ledger open on his lap, crunching numbers etc., and I was lucky if he ever said "Good Morning" to me.

Monnie would sit up front and was very cordial, asking me now and then where we were, how fast were we going, what time we would be in Grand Forks etc. Of course I'd always call fifteen minutes out so there would be a car there waiting for them. We'd always leave Duluth at 7:30 in the morning and not get back into Duluth until about 7:30 that same night. He'd even say, "Nice landing," once in awhile!

On this trip I asked Monnie if he'd mind if I got a day room at the Holiday Inn and they could call me there an hour before they wanted to leave. He asked me why I wanted to do that and I said so I can take a nap and a shower before we leave and be freshened up. "Besides, you don't want to be shooting an approach into Duluth, down to 200 and a 1/2 with a pilot who's been up and on his feet since 5:30 in the morning. It's unsafe. He asked how much it cost for a day room. I said, $7.00--maybe another five bucks for lunch. He said, no problem; do it. I sure felt a lot more alert flying back to Duluth that trip! I had gotten tired of standing around an airport all day!

The next day I was up at 5:30 again for another 7:30 takeoff in the 310 N5733Mike to Bemidji and back in the late afternoon. On the 18th I checked Roy Larson out in a Ercoupe! On the 22nd I had a charter in the "421" for Blandin Paper in Grand Rapids. The rest of the November I spent with my students.

On December 5th I started one of my best friends, Russ Johnston, on the instrument course! Russ was living in Ashland but had lived a block away from me when I owned Sunnyside Motel and Mobile Home Park in Cloquet. We had been in JC's together and Russ was an announcer on WKLK radio. He was one of those rare people that when you'd meet him he'd make you feel like you were the most important person on earth too!

On the 6th I had a charter in the "421" from Duluth to Grand Rapids, back to Duluth, and over to Oshkosh. We spent the night – no steaks and drinks though – and returned to Grand Rapids and Duluth the next day.

Russ was back on the 11th and we flew for 2.1 hours. He spent the night at my house and we did some ground-school work and then we shared a nice supper with him. The next morning we flew again for 1.4 hours and spent another hour on ground-school.

On the 13th I gave several rides in the "150" to East High School aviation students. There was only about 10 knots of wind on the ground but up at 2,500 feet it was blowing about 45 knots out of the west! But, it was really smooth! When I had the first student up and got leveled off at 2,500,

I looked down at the ground and it looked as though we were hardly moving! I asked the student, "Did they teach you that airplanes can back up?" He said, "No, airplanes can't back up!" While he was talking, I had throttled back and lowered the flaps. I said, "Look down at the ground. Looks like were going backwards to me." He looked down and said, "I can't believe it, we are backing up!"

When we landed, he got out and shouted to his teacher and the rest of the students, "That airplane can back up!" Of course I showed that to the next three students too! Before they left, their teacher explained to them why, the airplane was backing up. I'd had my fun though!

On the 16th I had a charter to Langdon, North Dakota in a 172! I had been there a couple of times already. Johnny Robertson was running the airport, instructing, crop spraying, selling fuel, etc. I was reading a magazine and Johnny was preparing his bills to send out. He handed me a bill and said, think this will work Les? It was a gas bill to some local guys for a few hundred dollars. Halfway down he had written, "pay up you sons-a-bitches!!" I said, it'll get their attention no doubt. They were obviously friends he could talk to that way. It was a long day in a 172 with 7.9 hours logged. We had left Duluth at 8:00 A.M. and didn't land back in Duluth until 8:00 that night! The next day I gave five more intro rides to East High students, but it wasn't windy so I couldn't back up!

On the 18th Russ was back and I checked him out in the 172 and flew that for 2.1 hours. We had used the 150 for the basic instrument work and now he was ready to start doing some ILS and ADF approaches.

On the 20th I flew Dr. Swenson up to International Falls in the "310" so he could do a few hours of surgery there. On the 21st I had another Charter with the Goldfines to Grand Forks and back. Same thing, have the left engine running and the right door open and they'd be getting in! Erv would sit in the back and crunch numbers and Monnie would sit up front and talk to me.

When we arrived, I had the airplane put into a heated hangar and I checked into the Holiday Inn. It was nice to take a hot tub, shower, have lunch, read the paper, take a nap and get a call from Monnie about an hour before they wanted to leave.

I had December 23rd, 24th and Christmas day off with the family which felt good! And as long as everyone, including me, was dressed up it was a good time to get a picture!

We went over to Cloquet to the wife's folks for Christmas Day. The food was always great and the drinks weren't bad either! What could I do? It was a holiday! Through the rest of the month I flew with my students Vic Thompson, Earl King, Tim Tyson, Bill Radke, Kerry Welsh, and Roy Larson.

On December 29th I had a charter to Cleveland Burke Lakefront Airport in our brand new 1971 Cessna 310, N 7646 Quebec! Was that ever nice! We flew to Cleveland in three hours! We spent the night and returned to Duluth the next day. Of course we had

The author, the wife, Rhonda, Timothy, LeeAnn and Keith, in order of age.

a headwind going back so it took 3.8 hours. N7646Quebec was new and beautiful. I loved flying her!

I started 1972 off by flying with Russ on New Years Day! We practiced VOR holding, 1 VOR approach, 1 ILS front course and 1 ILS back course approach.

On the 3rd Don Hudson was my first victim, I mean student of the day. Don always had a big smile and a lot of enthusiasm. Can I buy you a cup of coffee Les? No, you can't, in fact it ain't Les to you anymore, it's Mr Hubbell, in fact worse yet, it's examiner Hubbell to you!(God, I liked doing that to my students!) From now on I don't give a dam about you, your wife, your kids, how much money you've got, or what kind of a car you drive. All I want to know is, do you know the regulations, aircraft manual and can you fly the airplane! Sit down, this is your oral exam! Don made it through the oral so we went out to preflight 22 Golf. About everything he touched I asked, what is that and what does it do?? When he got to the prop I asked him what the red paint was for on the blade tips? He said, that's the red circle of danger. I said, it is not. He said, what is it then? I said, that red paint is there to keep the silver paint from sliding off at high RPM! Don just shook his head and smiled. He was probably wondering though how the hell I ever got an instructor rating! He finished the pre-flight and after starting up and getting taxi instructions we taxied out for takeoff. Again as he was doing the run-up I was asking what he was doing and why? What does this instrument do, what does that one do? Electric or vacuum?? Finally I let him complete his run-up and he got a take off clearance so we headed for the practice area. We reviewed ground reference maneuvers and then came back in and he made a nice soft field landing, so I got off his back! I flew with Ed Culbert in the afternoon for 1.3 hours and got home in time for supper! On the 4th, I flew with Kerry Welsh for 1.1, Tom Bucanan for .9 in the morning and after lunch I flew with Earl King for 1.5 and then Mike Gardonio for 1.5 hours doing an instrument takeoff with a XC (cross country) to Hibbing for a VOR hold and the back to Duluth for a ILS 9 approach. I always admired how Mike could hold a heading, altitude and airspeed etc. Sometimes I'd think, I wish I could do that good!! But then Mike had been a helicopter pilot in Vietnam and probably had a few hundred hours of that under his belt already. On the 5th I flew with with Kerry Welsh for a hour doing takeoffs and landings. And then Lew Gibbs for the first time. After lunch I flew with John Cartier for 1.3 hours and then Rick Alston for a instrument flight back up to Hibbing, held at the VOR and back to Duluth for the ILS 9 approach for another 1.5 hours! And when I got back there were some more East High students for intro rides so I did that for another 1.7 hours making the total for the day 6.3 hours! Figuring time for pre-flighting, post-flighting, lunch, and a couple of trips to the bathroom, that was a long day!

On the 6th Steve, the general manager came and told me they had to get a Skidoo part to Fargo ASAP for a race later that day. Halvorson's were also the Skidoo distributors for the upper mid-west so it was very important to get the part out there. Not important enough to take the new "310"though, just a "172" importance! So I signed out the 172 N4213Quebec. Mike Gardonio showed up for his lesson about the time I was ready to file IFR, being there were actual IFR conditions in the Duluth area and extending beyond Grand Rapids some. Mike suggested we just turn this trip into his lesson so I gave him a quick weather brief-ing, and discussed the route and altitude with him and had him file the IFR flight plan. Then he went out into the hangar and pre-flighted "13Quebec" and when he was fin-ished we opened the door and pulled her out, jumped in and started her up before the cockpit got cold! It was a very windy raw day! The winds were blowing out of the West at 20 knots and gusting! Mike called for taxi instructions, taxied out to the mid-field intersection on "27", copied his IFR clearance, did a run-up, got a takeoff clearance and we were in the air by the time he got full throttle pushed in!! The winds got stronger with altitude so we were going to be "low and slow". When we leveled off at "4 thousand" and Mike set up a cruise rpm of 2300 and leaned "13Quebec" out , we had a ground speed of 60 knots! I had him increase the rpm to 2500 and we picked up a few more knots, but not much! Fargo was 200 knots from Duluth so it was going to be a long day! I was thinking, I should have brought a lunch, and a pillow too!! At least it wasn't very bumpy, just slow! We had broke out on top at about 3,500 feet so we were out of the ice and the little bit we had picked up in the climb soon sublimated off. The weather cleared up just west of Grand Rapids as predicted and other than being slow, we were FDAH! (Fat Dumb And Happy) It took us about 3.3 hours to get to Fargo and I figured at that power setting and altitude we were burning about 9gallons a hour of fuel. The fuel gauges were bouncing around under the 1/4 tanks mark, which gave me a "pucker factor" of "point 8", plus my bladder was at a "point 9!" So when we got handed off to Fargo approach I had Mike cancel "IFR" and then contact the tower and we went "direct" to the airport and landed. (we of course had our 45 minutes of reserve fuel as required) We handed off the Skidoo part to a guy waiting for it, hit the bathroom, grabbed a couple of candy bars and a coke, fueled up, and filed back to DLH at 5,000ft. Now though we should have a ground speed of about 145 knots! Mike called and got a clearance and we were airborne within 10 minutes and on our way up to 5000 feet! We leveled off at "5" and eagerly watched as the DME kept spooling up and settled down on about 148kts. That extra thousand feet higher going back got us another 3 knots ground speed! I told Mike, "any faster and the wings will come off! He just looked at me like Don Hudson had when I told him what the red paint was for. One hour and about twenty minutes we were back to Duluth landing on "27!" It was windier when we got back than it was when we left! Mike landed and easily made the diagonal turnoff, which was covered with snow and ice, and taxied toward the tower. The wind was blowing so hard we had to let the airplane weather vane a little into the wind and apply enough power to keep it moving forward and not blown backwards off the taxiway! Mike had done a good job and had gotten some good experience so we did our "postflighting" over at the "Afterburner Club" down below the tower. What could I do, it was business! It had been a easy flight so we just did a "two beer postflight" and called it a day. The morning of the 7th I had 3 intro rides and after lunch I flew with Don Hudson for a hour. With the preflight and postflight discussions, that finished the day off. I wanted to get home a little early because Russ was driving up from Ashland and going to be spending the night with us. I spent all of the next morning with Russ in "ground school" and after lunch I had him file a "IFR" up to Hibbing. I put him under the hood and had him make a "ITO" off "27" and intercept the airway to Hibbing. We did the "VOR 31" approach at Hibbing and taxied in. We discussed the flight, grabbed a bite to eat and stopped onto "Flight Service" to get a weather up-date and then Russ filled out a IFR flight plan back to Duluth and turned it in. After a brief "pit stop" we went back out and Russ preflighted "13Quebec" for the return flight. He started up and called for a "airport advisory" and we taxied out. Soon FSS called with his "IFR" clearance and after a run-up he pulled out onto runway "31" and I handed him the hood again. He gave me that, "you jerk look" and I said, anyone can takeoff "VFR", "ITO's" separate the "men from the boys!" I knew, deep down though, that he liked "ITO's!" I kept him under the hood until the middle marker for runway 9 at Duluth and had him land with a little tailwind. With 10,000 plus feet to land on I figured it would be good experience for him to land with a little faster ground speed than what he was use to. We did a "3 beer " postflight over at the "Afterburner Club" and I headed home. As usual the kids and Ginger, the dog, were glad to see me but the wife hardly knew that I was home. I was getting a sickening feeling that I was married to the wrong woman for me. The 10th I took Dr Swenson down to Minneapolis in the new "310" N7646Quebec, and was back just after lunch. I always looked forward to flying "46Quebec!" Tom Bucanan was waiting for me when I got back so we went out in "28Golf" and spent 1.2 hours doing ground reference maneuvers and stalls. The next day I did a "XC" with Ed Sutton in the "172" to Minneapolis and back. On the 13th I had to do a, "part 135"check ride in "46 Quebec" that lasted 2.3 hours! On the 14th I gave Dr Swenson 2.8 hours of dual in the "310", N 3285X to International Falls and back. On the 17th I flew with Lou Gibbs and Roland Hanson. On the 18th I flew with a intro ride with Jim Carr in the morning and then took Mr Schumaker to Minneapolis in the "210", N9471Mike. For the next week I kept busy with Don Hudson, Roland Hanson, Russ Johnston, Lew Gibbs and Doug Peyton, except for the "22nd" when I flew up to Grand Rapids with Don Hudson so he could take his private check ride with Gordy Newstom. I could have signed him off for a solo XC but I liked Don and I hadn't seen Gordy for awhile so I decided to go with. Truth be known, I guess I just felt like, "goofing off" for awhile!! Don passed his check ride and was all smiles on the way back! He didn't look at me any-more like he was wondering how the hell I got a instructors rating!! That alone was worth the trip! Well, that and the fact that he bought the beer later at the Afterburner Club! On the 24th I took off for 5 days and drove down to "IFT" at the Minneapolis airport to start the "ATP" (Airline Transport Pilot) ground school course. I'd be at IFT all day studying and at night I had rented a room in a house near the airport with an elderly couple. I'd stop for a bite to eat and then when I got to my room I'd crawl in bed and study until 2-2:30 in the morning. I would just lose track of time when I was studying!!

When I got back I instructed Lew Gibbs and Russ Johnston for a couple of days and then back to "IFT" for another 5 days of "simulator" training. I had never been in one of those, "black boxes" before but it didn't take me long to figure out it was just one of those, "mind over matter" things. Actually it got to be a lot of fun! One time my instructor got called away for a phone call while I was in the simulator and he said to just do what I wanted for awhile, so I wrote my initials on the simulators tracking map before he got back! I was there from the 7th through the 10th and left feeling like I had learned a lot!

The rest of February and the first 6 days of March I was pretty busy with Russ, Mike, Goldfine's, Lew, Earl King, Al Pitoscia, Kerry Welsh, Doug Peyton, etc, etc. On the 7th of March I left again for "IFT" in Minneapolis for the "flight" portion of the "ATP." My instructor was Jack Donnell and we hit it off good from the start The trainer was a Piper Aztec, N751FT. I had never flown a Aztec before but it was like, "peaches and cream" on instruments, compared to the "310's" I was use to, especially on one engine! One day I had kind of screwed up getting into a holding pattern so when we got back to IFT Jack put me into the "simulator" so he could better show me what I should have done. We had covered what I had "screwed up" on and went on doing some other things and things were going pretty good until I, "lost my radios". I went back through all the frequencies as I could remember them, but I still wasn't getting my radios back so I dialed in 121.15 and tried that. Jack stuck his head in and said, what frequency is that Les? I said, that's my mother-in-law, she'll always tell me where to go! Jack said, you've got your radios back! Everything went well with the rest of the flight portion and Jack signed me off on March 11th for my check ride. I couldn't get with a FAA examiner until the 13th so I had a day off to relax before the check-ride! The morning of the 13th I preflighted N751FT" and taxied over near the tower where the GADO office was. The examiner was Ned Powers. Ned asked me where I was from and what I did etc. Turned out he was from Grand Rapids, Minnesota and of course knew Gordy Newstrom. I assumed Ned would be just like me when I played the examiner part with my students. Well, actually he wasn't a "prick" like I was when I played examiner with my students. That's why all my students would come back from their checkrides and say, "that examiner was no where near as mean as you are Les!" I'd say, yes, but did he let you buy him coffee, or did he just want to know if you knew the regulations, the manual and could you fly the airplane?" I still knew parts 61 and 91's verbatim and had part 135 down pretty good! Ned asked me several IFR questions etc and then we went out and he asked some more questions about the Aztec as I pre-flighted it. After I started up and talked to "ground" we taxied over to the run-up area for "11 left". While I was taking my "sweet time" doing the run-up, using a checklist of course, a FAA "nav check" Gooney Bird, (DC3) taxied in behind me to the right. He did a quick run-up and I heard him call "ground" to taxi for takeoff. The "ground controller" asked him if he had room to get by the Aztec? He said, "oh ya" and I'm looking back thinking, "bullshit!" He was going to be putting his left wing right over my right engine! Granted there still might be a foot or two of clearance, but just to be on the safe side I shut the right engine down and flattened the prop. As he taxied by I asked Ned, "isn't that a little close for a FAA airplane?? Ned said, "that's a little to close for any airplane." as he wrote something in ink on his hand. (*Hmmm, could it have been a "N" number, I thought?*)

After that I felt I couldn't do to much wrong! I even asked Ned if he wanted a "ITO!" He said, "no, let's wait until we've got a couple hundred feet of altitude. I put the hood on when Ned told me to and he gave me heading and altitude instructions to the south and about ten miles out he asked for some steep turns, left and right, a stall and then a holding pattern at a intersection. Then he told me to intersect a airways etc and after I was established on that he gave me a altitude and heading toward Crystal airport. About 5 miles away he handed me a small piece of note pad that he had scribbled an approach on for the Crystal airport off the WCCO 830Am radio tower. He asked if I could fly that? I said, yes, I can and thought to myself, "I'm glad there ain't any wind to amount to anything though!!" I contacted Crystal tower and told them what we were doing and flew the approach as he had drawn it. When I called the missed approach point he said, "look up" and I'll be dammed, there was the airport!! There's nothing like a little, "Luck of the Irish" once in awhile I thought!! From there he had me call MSP approach and tell them we were a checkflight and request vectors for the ILS 04. It was an absolutely perfect day for a checkride, not a bump and CAUV!! The only way that Aztec would get off altitude or heading is if I wanted it to!! I got to the outer marker for "04" at MSP and Ned said, "ah, take your hood off!" I knew I had passed!! Of course on a day like that who could fail!! I even got luckier and "kissed" that Aztec onto the runway!! We went in and Ned typed up the paper work and congratulated me on doing a good job. God, I felt good leaving there!! I started up and taxied back over to IFT and shut down. When I got to the glass door going into the office there was a "Snoopy" cartoon that Jack had drawn, saying "Congratulations Captain Les!" It was signed by Jack and everyone else at IFT!

It has hung in my office and home every since. It will always be one of my most treasured possessions!! All I

Within the image: CONGRATULATIONS CAPTAIN LES ! IT MAKES ONE PRO Knew you'd make it. Jack Donnell

"Snoopy", by Jack Donnell"

could think of on the drive back to Duluth was, I'm a multi-engine Airline Transport Pilot!! In fact I'm a multi-engine Airline Transport pilot with a instructor rating, single engine sea, single engine land, and instrument rating!! And I've never flunked a written or a check ride along the way!! And so far none of my students have flunked a written or check ride either!! I really did some serious thinking on the two and a half hour drive back home. I thought, I graduated from high school without ever taking a book home, I was second in my class at aircraft mechanics school at Sheppard Air Force base, I got the highest score ever made in the Air Force on the 43151B test over on Okinawa, I got the highest score on the flight engineers test at Bolling Air Force base, I designed and built a mobile home park when I was about 25 years old, I built the furniture in Sunnyside Motel in 1961, and it's still there, and now I've just passed the Airline

Transport Pilot flight test! I thought, (Hmmm, I must not be the "dumbest kid in the world"!!) I wonder, (Hmmm, Maybe I'm just the luckiest kid in the world??!!)

Book Two to be continued with:

It Don't Pay to be Perfect!

Quitting my Job!

Starting my Seventh Career Change!

Watching Two People Burn in a 182!

Taking off from Grand Rapids, MN on the Snow January 1st, 1973 with a 185-on-Floats and Delivering it to Florida!

Landing a 180-on-Floats on a restricted lake in Akron, Ohio!

Moving to Arizona!

Flying Gliders!

Moving Back to Minnesota!

My Oldest Brother wishes me, Dead in an Airplane!

One of my Best Friends Dies in an Airplane that he Bought from Me.

My First Affair!

My First Divorce!

My Second Divorce!

Getting Sued by my First Divorce Attorney and a Doctor Friend!

Finding out, I'm Not the Luckiest Kid in the World Either!

Thanks and Credits

I give thanks and credit, to my parents (both deceased) for raising me.(instead of sending me to reform school!)

I give thanks and credit, to the United Sates Airforce for turning me from a boy into a man. And for testing me and determining what my areas of aptitude were. And for training me in those areas. And for all the travel I got to do, by train, boat and planes, to places that I'd never had gotten to, if I hadn't joined the Air Force!

I give thanks and credit to Tech Sergeant DelRoy Mills, Staff Sergeants; Bruce Currie(deceased), Ronald (Rex) Young, Rhuel Sperry, Joe Dungan and Louis Ajan (deceased). Without the help and training I received from these sergeants, I would have never become a "flight engineer" for the "Vice Chief' of Staff's Office!"

I give thanks and credit to Carl and Lillian Bystrom (both deceased) for loaning $9000 to the wife and me to buy Sunnyside Motel and Trailer Park. Without their loan I'd never had all the fun I did building a new Mobile Home Park and the furniture in Sunnside Motel, and my "inventions!" Without the Motel and Mobile Home Park I'd never been able to afford to take the flying lessons and buy the airplanes that eventually led me to becoming an "Airline Transport Pilot!"

I give thanks and credit to Patricia "Trish" Stoch from Duluth for editing this book! Trish is a retired English teacher, and I imagine my abuse of the English language, and my typing have driven her, "about halfway to drink!"

I give thanks and credit to Johnson and Peggy, and to the whole Johnson family for their friendship, the pheasant hunting and all the great meals I've had over the years! I give additional thanks to Johnson for the great pictures he donated for this book!

I give Thanks and credit to Duede for being a great roommate on Okinawa and for the great pictures he donated to this book! But I wonder, (Hmmm, what kind of sicko would keep a picture of someone vomiting for 46 years!!) Thanks Duede!

And last, but not least, I give thanks and credit, as I do about ten times a day, to God for looking down and "saving my bacon" so many times!! And also for my health, and happiness, without which, I wouldn't have been able to do much of anything!

THANK YOU ALL!!
Leslie V. Hubbell
"Your Average Aircraft Salesman"